The
Budget Garden

Creating a
Beautiful Garden at
Minimum Cost

MARION CURRY

JAVELIN BOOKS

LONDON · NEW YORK · SYDNEY

To the man who bought my first spade
To the girl who tied a red ribbon round it and
To the baby who allowed me to write about it.

First published in the UK 1988 by Javelin Books,
an imprint of Cassell plc,
Artillery House, Artillery Row, London sw1p 1rt

Copyright © 1988 Marion Curry

Distributed in the United States by
Sterling Publishing Co., Inc.,
2 Park Avenue, New York, NY 10016

Distributed in Australia by
Capricorn Link (Australia) Pty Ltd,
PO Box 665, Lane Cove, NSW 2066

British Library Cataloguing in Publication Data

Curry, Marion
   The budget garden : creating a beautiful
   garden at minimum cost.
   1. Gardens. Planning
   I. Title
   712'.6

ISBN 0 7137 2024 7

Typeset by Inforum Ltd, Portsmouth

Printed and bound in Great Britain by Adlard & Son Ltd, Letchworth, Herts.

CONTENTS

ACKNOWLEDGEMENTS

Obviously no book exists in isolation and *The Budget Garden* is no exception. In addition to the books listed in the Bibliography, which I found particularly useful for this project, there is another list at least twice as long of other books which I have also enjoyed and which were an indirect source of inspiration.

Numerous gardening magazines, television and radio programmes and newspaper articles have also yielded copious information. I also acknowledge a debt to gardening friends who have passed on their own money-saving tips.

FOREWORD

This book aims to put a beautiful garden within everyone's reach, at the minimum possible cost. Throughout, the emphasis is on getting the maximum effect for the smallest outlay while enjoying the task at the same time.

In addition to a whole chapter of money saving ideas and economical tips, there are suggestions on the best tools to buy and where they can be bought most cheaply. For instance, did you know about the bargains to be had at auction, or the mysteries of a car boot sale?

Gardening beginners are helped to design their own gardens without making costly mistakes and the essentials of the various garden styles are discussed.

The basics of soil preparation, planting and ways of increasing plants are also covered without resort to unintelligible 'gardenese' and a glossary is included to provide a speedy double check on any essential horticultural terms not found in everyday speech.

INTRODUCTION: 'DO TREES REALLY COST THAT MUCH?'

Armed with an extensive shopping list, the initial trip to a garden centre can be a frightening business. 'Do trees really cost that much?' 'I didn't realise spades were so expensive', and 'We could only afford a couple of geraniums', are common enough reactions, particularly if starting a garden for the first time.

Moving house is when most people take on a new plot or plan major garden renovations. This is an expensive time for everyone. Unexpected expenses crop up and your dream home often costs more than first envisaged. When there are so many other demands on a household's income it is easy to see why some people feel the garden must take a backseat. A garden, however, is an important part of the overall appearance of a house. It is permanently on show, helps create the first impression of your home and should be seen as an extra room or living area which complements your home. Your garden deserves as much attention as other parts of your house because a neglected tangle of weeds never did anything for anyone.

As the cost of a new carpet for the sitting room vies with the desire to plant up your new garden, don't accept the thought that there is no alternative to leaving large patches of bare earth. Instead of being daunted by that unappealing patch of builder's rubble, see it as a challenge – to create maximum effect for minimum cost.

Admittedly if you decided to buy all your gardening needs – plants, tools, and construction materials – brand new you would be faced with a hefty bill, which might even make your bank manager's eyes water. Garden centres and plant nurseries, however, cannot be made out the villains of the piece. Established plants by their very natures can be expensive to produce. This is particularly true of the less hardy and slower growing plants, such as some of the shrubs and trees. Tools, too, have to be seen as long term investments, as treated properly they can last a lifetime.

Even if you are setting up home for the first time and have to start buying tools from scratch there are many ways to cut costs in gardening without sacrificing quality or variety. Fortunately, not all gardens need cost a fortune and this book aims to help beginner gardeners avoid costly mistakes, while making the most of their resources both economically and horticulturally.

More experienced gardeners may also enjoy the money saving ideas, as I am sure that within all true gardeners there is a love of getting 'something for nothing'. After all, isn't it magical when seeds costing only a few pence turn into beautiful blooms brightening up summer borders and providing lovely posies for the house?

1   **GARDEN PLANNING**

SETTING THE STYLE

You will probably already have a rough idea of how you want your garden to look. However, before buying any plants and before laying or redesigning the lawn it is worth considering the general style of garden you admire.

You are more likely to achieve a garden with which you are happy if you get the basics correct from the beginning. Obviously no garden is ever 'finished', as keen gardeners are never completely satisfied with their work. There are always new plants to include and different planting designs to try — that's part of the fun: but if you work from within a sound framework, your garden should develop and mature in a way that pleases you. It is very discouraging to go to the expense and trouble of planting an area which, once finished, you feel is a disappointment. Moreover, if you are constantly redoing areas, they do not have time to mature and the garden always has a raw or unfinished look.

There are numerous different styles of garden, including the architectural, basically easy upkeep garden, the vegetable garden, the summer garden, the wild garden and the cottage garden. You may like a particular style of garden which you wish to emulate, or if you have a large garden you may want to incorporate two or three different kinds of garden within the whole. Alternatively you could choose to take different aspects from various styles to make a delightful mix unique to yourself. After all, the different kinds of garden, while being distinct, are not mutually exclusive.

THE ARCHITECTURAL GARDEN

If you have a small garden in which there is little ground space for planting or you have little time to spend maintaining borders you may favour the so-called 'architectural' garden. This type of garden, which is very much in vogue at the moment, concentrates on making the maximum use of available room by providing a mixture of plants within a framework of hard materials.

The architectural garden may sound very grand but in practice it simply means creating strong visual effects with plants, usually within relatively small areas. A lawn may be excluded altogether, and the space used instead for a paved sitting area with paths to allow access to planted areas. Bold plants such as the false castor oil are used to increase interest and enliven the possibly hard appearance of paving. Garden statues are sometimes mysteriously hidden amongst foliage or prominently displayed in the form of a bird bath or sun dial. Raised beds, which are the essence of such gardens, are also popular, not only because they can be features in themselves but because they provide more and varied levels of planting.

Raised Beds

Raised beds, which can be fairly easily and cheaply constructed to provide a dramatic visual effect, give you the opportunity for growing a variety of plants, not only in the bed, but tumbling out of it and clinging to its walls. Filled with soil altered by the addition of peat you could even grow acid-loving heathers in an area with a limey soil which they cannot tolerate.

Plants can be used to cascade down the sides and even very common species such as aubretia can look wonderful in the spring as the varied shades of purple and mauve flowers bloom. Plants such as houseleek and cushion saxifrage may even be introduced into the actual sides of the bed, to create even greater interest.

Trees and Climbers

It is important to have a few plants growing above the level of fencing to draw the eye away from what could be a rather daunting line, but it is imperative to choose such plants carefully. While a weeping willow might look majestic beside a boating lake in the local park it will not do much in the average suburban garden, except undermine the house foundations. If you can only have one tree it must be reasonably compact and pay its way in terms of year-long interest. A tree may have beautiful spring blossom, but if that is its only merit it cannot command a place in the small garden.

Two trees that are favourites of mine, suited to small gardens, are the June berry (*Amelanchier canadensis*) and the mountain ash (*Sorbus* 'Joseph Rock'). The former grows about ten feet high and is an attractive small tree suited to damp and semi-shade. It has lovely autumn colour and small white flowers in the spring, which are followed by black berries. The *Sorbus* grows about twenty-five feet high, has beautiful leaves which vary from red through to almost purple in the autumn with long lasting yellow berries to follow.

Climbing plants are another feature of the architectural garden as they provide yet another way of making full use of a small space. Foliage and flowers can climb up and over walls and fences to soften harsh outlines and hide eyesores. Plants like clematis can be grown up and through the branches of a tree to provide added interest when the host is past its best show. Ivies too, in their myriad of forms, can be used to climb, hang down or creep along the ground. They vary in colour from the deepest of forest greens to bright yellows and every variegated combination in between, so are not plants to be dismissed as being too common to be of interest. Their other great value is in being self-clinging which means they need no help to climb.

Scented climbing plants such as the easy-going honeysuckle are wonderful used around house windows and outdoor seating areas where their perfume can be appreciated.

Bulbs Having considered height it is important not to neglect that which is often hidden underneath the soil for much of the year, namely bulbs. A serious study of nursery catalogues will provide you with a list of goodies such as snowdrops, muscari, narcissus, tulips, lilies and autumn crocus with which to underplant other plants in your garden to ensure a good show throughout the year.

Container Plants Plants grown in containers give yet another planting possibility. Because containers can be moved indoors at the first sign of frost, unlike raised beds which are *in situ* all year round, you can introduce fairly exotic plants such as the non-hardy yucca and the date palm.

Large plant containers in terracotta or stone can be expensive to buy, so it is worth checking out the local auction centre. Often when there is a sale from a large house or estate such pots and urns are sold at very competitive prices. These pots have an extra quality, being aged and weathered by the elements, which is much nicer than modern imitations.

As an alternative to buying one large pot you could think about grouping together a number of smaller pots growing a variety of plants of differing heights for impact. Small terracotta pots are really quite cheap to buy as they do not have to be hand thrown; however, because they dry out more quickly than their plastic counterparts, you may have to water them as often as twice a day in summer. Coupled with the disadvantage of having to water them frequently is the danger of their cracking during hard frosts if left outside during winter. These I see as minor considerations, however, as terracotta's good looks far outweigh the more practical advantages plastic might have.

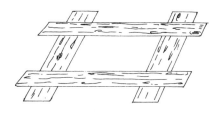

An easily-constructed wooden cover to hide a plastic tub

A good compromise, particularly if you want a large container at little cost is to use a large plastic bucket of the sort in which builder's putty is kept. Such buckets are usually discarded by glaziers and builders and you might like to try approaching them for one. Simply drill a number of holes in the bottom for drainage and construct a wooden outer casing to hide the plastic. A slatted wooden cover can be easily made by building up a two on two system of wooden slats, nailing them together and treating them with a non-toxic wood preserver.

Vegetables and Fruit

Having considered the various ways of using plants to give ground cover, height and maximum interest, do not forget that even in an architectural garden you need not deny yourself the bonus of fresh produce. Vegetables can be used to provide a dash of the unusual simply by mixing them into flower or foliage borders. Alternatively you could try growing potatoes in a barrel or strawberries in hanging baskets outside the kitchen door. Herbs are useful too for the kitchen and if you start with the trusted favourites such as marjoram, rosemary and parsley you will find them attractive and easy to grow in a border.

To give height as well as colour you could grow a wigwam of scarlet flowering runner beans on a framework of bamboo canes. By clever use of such canes you can arrange frames to mask unsightly views or fences, but ensure that your beans will not be subjected to too much wind damage.

With their great sprawling leaves and golden yellow flowers, courgettes are attractive enough to front any flower border, or you might like to try artichokes with their statuesque leaves, red cabbages with their deep shiny purple heads or chives with their dainty purple pom-pom heads. All of these plants can be used to complement an existing flower or foliage garden and whether you decide to try them purely as an experiment or as a means of increasing the visual interest in your garden you will have the satisfaction of being able to eat the fruits of your labours.

To Summarise

An architectural garden, with its emphasis on hard materials for paving and building, can mean a heavy initial expense. You can, of course, set against this the saving on the cost of a lawnmower and the man hours which need not be spent on the upkeep of a lawn.

Ease of maintenance is perhaps the greatest type of saving offered by the architectural garden. You will not need to devote every weekend to labouring in the garden: an advantage not only to those on a tight schedule but also those who are perhaps less capable of physical work, such as the elderly or infirm. Because, too, the idea of large areas of grass have been abandoned you have the chance to grow a variety of interesting plants. This is an obvious bonus in a small garden where space is tight.

It is particularly important to think carefully about which plants to use where space is limited and rather than buy a number of small relatively anonymous-looking plants, it is perhaps better to spend the same amount of money on one striking specimen. A bold plant commands attention and makes a dramatic impact. If you cannot afford enough plants to sufficiently cover a given area, plump for one large and spectacular specimen and let a ground covering and spreading ivy do the rest. Having said this it is important not to consider plants in isolation of course, as they should ideally either complement or provide a vivid contrast with their neighbours. The emphasis should always be on a successful mix of plants: a harmony of plants interspersed with a contrasting shape or colour to bring the garden to life.

Your idea of a 'proper' garden may be completely different from the architectural garden with its tendency towards the bold and dramatic within a fairly formal framework of hard materials. You may have set your heart on a vegetable garden with dreams of growing prize leeks, show onions and organically grown spuds, so with this in mind the next type of garden to look at is the vegetable garden.

THE VEGETABLE GARDEN

You may view a vegetable garden as the ultimate in getting something for nothing. If you do, a word of caution: I think you may be in for a rather nasty shock. Dreams of a smiling family being well fed on the produce of their own land are often tainted by reality.

The Drawbacks A vegetable garden very often means a great deal of work feeding and maintaining the soil at a level which will sustain production, a continuing effort to keep weeds at bay and an unstinting campaign against attack from the animal kingdom. You will probably find that everything that can creep, crawl, slither, slide, walk, burrow or fly into your garden will do so with one intent in mind – to feed on your crops.

This could mean that unless you are careful or lucky, your potato patch gives a less than worthy crop of maggot-infested potatoes, your gooseberry bushes are attacked by caterpillars which completely strip the branches and your cabbages disappear under the ravages of a slug attack.

Even if you do manage to harvest the fruits of your labours you could find yourself with a glut of vegetables no-one wants to eat. There is after all a limit to how many salads even the most helpful family can eat in one day. As you can't eat them or even give them away your crop quickly goes from maturity to seed and returns to the compost heap. All this at a time when the vegetables could probably have been bought with a lot less effort and perhaps less cost from your local greengrocer or supermarket.

The Bonuses If all this hasn't completely destroyed your vision of vegetable gardening, you can begin to count the benefits. You can save money by choosing to grow 'gourmet' vegetables such as mange-tout or sugar snap peas, fennel and, if you are patient, asparagus, which are expensive to buy in the shops.

Clever planning and staggered planting will also provide you with vegetables outside their normal season; for example, you could plan to provide the family with a picking of new potatoes for the table on Christmas Day or you might like to force on a head of early rhubarb.

If you have a freezer you can of course cope with glut harvests with impunity. Crops like beans and peas freeze well, as do fruits like red and blackcurrants. But for me the real pleasure of vegetable gardening is eating the produce almost straight from the bush. You know how your plants have been grown, and you can ensure, if you choose to, that they are free from any chemical applications. Nothing can be fresher than that which is picked and on the table within minutes.

The difference in price between shop-bought and home-grown tomatoes may be minimal, but only one can offer the experience of the warm, sweet, almost effervescent smell which arises when you pick a tomato from the mother plant. It really is the stuff from which memories are made! And while you might justify growing potatoes on the grounds that it saves you hefting them back from the shops it is hard to surpass a child's amazement on first seeing the 'treasure' of potatoes growing beneath the unexciting stalks. Even if you haven't the space or inclination to grow a patch of potatoes it is worth letting a child plant just a couple in a bucket. Allow him to look after them by watering and feeding them and follow it through until the finished article arrives on his plate – as all his own work.

Whatever you intend to grow, in either the fruit or vegetable line be realistic. Only grow crops which are feasible. Don't for instance attempt to grow carrots, which prefer a light sandy soil, if you have heavy clay as you are only asking for disappointment. Nor should you grow vegetables just because you can – if you find spinach does very well on your ground but no-one likes to eat it, again you will be frustrated.

Finally, it is worth selecting between different types of particular vegetables as some are more suited to particular soils, give better yields and are generally more worth while than others. I find early potatoes delicious and certainly worth growing but maincrop potatoes, which mature later and take up the same amount of space, a waste of time. I think you are better devoting the ground to other vegetables at that time.

Growing Conditions If you decide to go ahead with a vegetable garden, how you tackle it rather depends on the space available to you. Ideally the ground should be in a fairly sheltered spot, open to the sun with a little shade, not overhung by trees, and the soil free draining. However, even where your growing conditions are

However, even where your growing conditions are far less favourable, if you take care in selecting your vegetables, start them off as seeds, plant them out in prepared ground and perhaps give them a sheltered start in a cloche, there need be no limit on what you can achieve.

Cultivation

Neatly serried ranks of vegetables grown in precisely drawn drills may appeal to you, and a traditional vegetable plot can indeed look very attractive but it does call for attention to detail and tidiness. Approximating distances and straight lines is not enough and will not give you the desired appearance. To achieve a military type of neatness, draw drills by stretching a length of garden twine between two wooden pegs and then draw the edge of a hoe along the string and soil. To make a shallow drill for tiny seeds it is often enough simply to press down the handle of a hoe onto the soil along the length of the string. This will give you a narrow indentation into which you can sow seeds, covering them by simply pinching the soil over with your fingers.

When planting out young seedlings or indeed planting large seeds like peas it is useful to use a marked board. Any old piece of wood will do as long as it is reasonably straight and smooth. Mark one side off clearly into six inch intervals using a permanent marker pen. You now have an accurate gauge for spacing plants and seeds. You might think it unimportant whether there is a five inch or a six inch gap between seeds but they all need their own growing spaces, and a slapdash approach when planting can never be rectified later and will spoil the neat appearance of the plot.

If you arrange the crops with a thought to size, shape and colour you can achieve attractive results. Consider the slender shape of leeks and onions contrasted with the rounds of lettuce and cabbage, or feathery leafed carrot tops acting as a foil to pyramids of scarlet flowering runner beans.

Scrap wood can make a useful planting aid

Deep Beds

Vegetables grown in the traditional allotment or patch method, however, are not the only possibility. You might prefer growing them on a deep bed system where the growing areas are split up into lengths not much broader than about four foot with walkways between. The soil to be cultivated is deeply dug with as much compost and manure worked in as possible. This not only improves the fertility of the soil but helps it become a more free draining and attractive growing medium. Moreover, because you need never walk on the soil but tend it from the walkways, either standing or kneeling or sitting for close hand weeding, you do not risk compacting the soil.

Because their breadth is limited by how far you can comfortably reach across them to tend them, I find these deep beds give a particular sense of fulfilment. You can easily tackle a bed and see the results of your labours in isolation from the rest of the garden. It is perhaps, then, an especially good way of starting a vegetable garden when you are beginning a garden from scratch, as it allows you to establish small areas at a time.

The deep bed system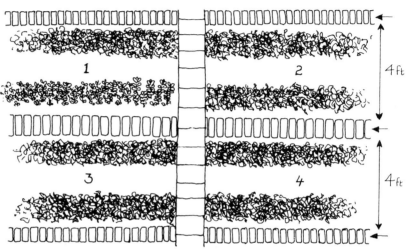

The walkways between beds need be no more than wooden planks placed alongside the beds or could be made from discarded stones and rubble uncovered while digging. They need not waste much space, being simply broad enough to walk on and wheel a barrow over. However, you might prefer more decorative paths made from grass and edged with narrow slabs to allow you to mow easily along their lengths. To make life easier for yourself, if you do choose to make such paths judge their width according to the width of your mower.

Screening Vegetable Beds   Vegetable gardens, particularly where part of a larger garden, can be attractively screened from the house by training fruit trees or bushes along a pre-established framework of wire and stakes or wooden trellis. Frames or screens, of course, give the additional bonus of fruit while making maximum use of available space. If you plan to start such a fruit screen you can buy already trained fruit from any reputable nurseryman, but it is often cheaper and easier to buy young fruit plants which you can gradually tie and prune into shape as they grow.

You may prefer a more consciously ornamental approach to vegetable gardening. After all, just because the display is provided by vegetables there is no need to give up on achieving an especially attractive garden.

The arrangement of paving or walkways in a garden mainly or wholly devoted to vegetables is important so it is worth considering different designs. Pictures of old knot gardens may be an inspiration to you. These gardens used intricate geometric patterns for planting, edging and delineating the growing beds with miniature hedges of box and herbs, which were carefully pruned to maintain their shape.

Alternatively you might like something simpler and easier to achieve. If you base your design on an old cartwheel with an external circular path, subdivided by single walkways to form the spokes of a wheel, you have the basis of a lovely pattern, with numerous beds for planting.

Even in a vegetable garden it is important to include somewhere to sit, either to rest from your labours or simply to enjoy the scents and pleasures of your garden. If you choose to carry out the wheel design, you might like to make room for a bench and table right in the middle, or hub, so you can sit surrounded by your garden like a spider in a web or you may prefer to find a shaded area off to one side. Either way, if you are to sit surrounded by vegetables think carefully about those to be used nearest the sitting area. After all, no matter how fond you are of spuds no one really wants to sit surrounded by them!

Herbs

Herbs are a useful addition to any garden and make neat and attractive edges to a vegetable garden as well as increasing the amount of foliage, colour and variety of scents. The sages, apart from being very useful in the kitchen come in a number of colours from the strongly growing variegated variety of green and creamy white through to a dark purple green. Chervil with its lovely lacey leaf grows well in the shade and makes a handsome edging plant. The thymes, when crushed underfoot give off a delightful scent and are good for interplanting amongst paving stones to soften a harsh appearance.

Hyssop is attractive and neat with its purple flowers and is a useful plant for attracting butterflies, as is marjoram, which provides a good show from late summer on of delicate pink flowers which would not disgrace any flower border.

Rue is a beautiful plant with its neat shape and distinctive blue-grey-green foliage. Chives are neat, cheerful and ever useful, as is garlic. Garlic can be slotted into any available sunny spot, even under roses where it is thought to spur on their growth.

Whatever you decide to grow and however you design your vegetable plot you will undoubtedly want to raise your own plants from seed. You can of course buy small plants in trays which only need to be transplanted and grown on to maturity but this can be expensive, and you can achieve just as good results much more cheaply by growing your own seeds.

Hyssop

Sowing   Most vegetable seed packets give very detailed instructions on cultivation and if you follow these strictly you should succeed. If you are a complete beginner, however, it might be wiser to start with the simpler things: for example, go for beans rather than asparagus and lettuce rather than celery.

Many of the seeds such as radish, lettuce, spinach and peas can be sown directly into prepared ground, but even with such stalwart seeds you will have failures. Even if they don't really need any special cossetting I prefer to start nearly all seeds off in seed trays, which gives them a better start and cuts down on losses. If you only have a few seed trays to sow you can easily do this in the house, using the airing cupboard to give an extra boost to those seeds which need a little warmth to germinate. When the seeds break through the surface of the soil you can keep them on a light windowsill to bring them on before finally hardening them off for planting outside.

On a small scale this works quite well, but it can become a bit of a bind, even to the dedicated gardener, to have every available windowsill crammed full of plant trays. If you are really keen you will probably start to hanker after a greenhouse, which will give you greater scope and allow you to grow a greater range of plants, from cucumbers to grapes, and melons.

To Summarise   The vegetable garden, then, is really for the keen gardener who wants to spend a great deal of leisure time in the garden. You have to be prepared to work the soil regularly, keep weeds to a minimum, and carefully tend growing plants. And while your expenses will be considerably more than the cost of a few packets of seed, if successful you will recoup your costs at harvest time both in terms of the crops themselves and the satisfaction of 'growing your own'.

If, however, you feel this type of garden is not for you either because you live alone and could not possibly cope with the quantity of produce, or because you prefer a more boisterously coloured garden, you might consider the summer bedding garden.

THE SUMMER BEDDING GARDEN

As the name suggests, the summer bedding garden concentrates its energy on a blazing display over the summer months. Because it can even be confined to hanging baskets and plant containers, this type of garden is suitable where space is extremely tight. Your garden may be no more than a backyard, patio or balcony but your enjoyment of it will undoubtedly be increased if you can see and smell a variety of flowers while sitting in the summer sun. Bedding schemes can

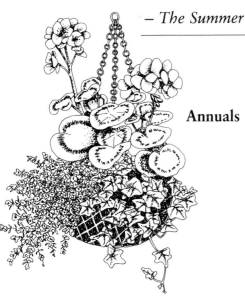

also be used to brighten larger gardens, without necessarily recalling the rather formal and regimented Victorian park schemes.

Annuals

Annuals, that is those plants which grow, flower and die all in one year, form the basis of all bedding schemes. You grow fresh plants for each summer and so have all the fun of poring over seed catalogues, comparing the merits of the almost infinite variety of flowers, making your selection and growing your own plants.

With the summer bedding garden you can be as bold and adventurous as you like in your planting schemes, as no experiment will be a disaster that you have to put up with for very long. You could try the bright and patriotic colours of red, white and blue with geraniums, lobelia and salvia, or you might prefer more subtle muted shades such as those offered by tobacco plants and cornflowers. Alternatively you might like the vast array of golds and yellows offered by marigolds and sunflowers. Whether you plan your own imaginative scheme or follow suggestions from seed catalogues, there is no shortage of choice amongst annuals.

Buying Annuals

Many summer annuals or bedding plants are sold in trays ready for planting out by garden centres and markets, but you will pay much more for one tray, holding perhaps five plants, than you will for a packet of seeds which may contain over one hundred potential plants. It is undoubtedly tempting to buy these ready-made plants because they are both easy and attractive in their various colours but if you do this on a large scale the costs will be high. It is much better to content yourself with buying only those plants necessary to fill your containers, window boxes and hanging baskets, where the instant display they provide is worth the cost.

Container Plants

Traditional favourites and good buys for containers are mixtures of geraniums, fuchsia and lobelia. These plants have both upright and trailing forms and come in a dazzling array of colours. Don't skimp on filling your containers: use a good compost and pack them full for maximum effect. Better to have just one container overflowing luxuriantly than two or three pots rather frugally planted.

For the rest of the garden, plan on growing your own annuals and biennials. You will get far more choice and it is a great deal more satisfying than simply slotting bought plants into place.

Sowing

Easiest of all seeds are those which are sown directly into prepared soil where they are to bloom. Amongst this large group I would always choose cornflowers, which are useful

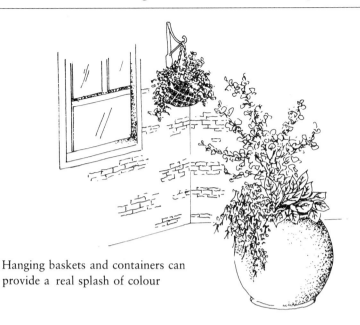

Hanging baskets and containers can provide a real splash of colour

both for their height (up to about four feet) and their variety of gentle colours; love-in-a-mist, because of its feathery foliage; poppies, nasturtiums, and virginian stock and candytuft. Children love growing sunflowers because they grow so quickly and have the extra advantage of being useful for feeding the birds in the winter. Marigolds are also popular with children as they grow so easily, provide lovely patches of gold and frequently set seed for next year if you are not too vigorous at weeding.

Seeds which benefit from being started off with a little warmth but which are certainly worth the trouble are those of the tobacco plants, for their perfume, *Cosmos*, as it is reliable, tall growing and comes in a number of good strong colours, and Busy Lizzie which is invaluable for those shady areas of the garden, where its bright colours can lift the shadows.

Biennials Even if you include biennials – that is those plants which are started from seed one year for flowering the next, like canterbury bells and foxgloves – a garden made up mainly from bedding plants has no permanent framework. This need not matter if your garden really is only a tiny backyard and you are concerned only to soften a few harsh outlines with hanging baskets and add a splash of moveable colour in containers for the summer. If, on the other hand, you want to enjoy your garden during the other seasons of the year, and want it to take on a maturity and changing perspective over the years you should consider a mainstay of easy-to-care-for shrubs. These will provide structure and interest when the bedding plants are not in flower without necessarily needing a lot of attention themselves. The framework being set, you can then indulge yourself in a riot of summer plants.

Shrubs There is a vast array of shrubs available so whatever the problems in your garden you should be able to find a plant which will do well. Some shrubs are particularly suited to shaded areas, others do best in dry sunny spots, while yet others favour the damp.

To narrow down the almost overwhelming choice of shrubs available think about your soil first of all. If you have a non-acid soil don't plump for acid-loving shrubs, like rhododendron, if you want an easy life. This is not to say you could never grow a rhododendron, as it would be possible by creating a special peat bed, but I hardly think it is worth the trouble. It is far easier to work with, rather than against, nature. Go for something which favours the conditions you have to offer: you can then reasonably hope the plant will thrive without any special labour on your part.

When choosing shrubs, take into account the eventual height and spread of fully grown plants. There is always a temptation to plant too closely together as initially young plants can look rather sad and forlorn in a sea of earth. Sooner or later however, you will pay for overplanting, when shrubs start crowding one another, destroying each other's shape and spoiling growth. You then have to face facts, admit your mistake and remove some of the plants. You should in any case leave room for planting your annual flowers between and not simply in front of shrubs in order to lead the eye in and out of the various contours of the garden, with hidden delights becoming visible as you stroll around the garden.

Any good nurseryman's catalogue will supply you with a great deal of basic information on height, favoured position, colour and timing of flowering and any special needs of shrubs. Don't neglect or despise the common shrubs simply for being popular, as their popularity is often due to the proven evidence of their hardiness and attractiveness, as well as ease of cultivation.

Amongst my favourite popular shrubs are the large family of potentilla. They are easy to grow, long flowering (from May to September) and come in a wide variety of colours from bright yellow buttercup-like flowers to mellow pink and rosy red. They are generally compact shrubs which grow up to about four feet high but there are also a number of very good low-growing types which make excellent ground cover.

The viburnum family also provide a good variety of shrubs to choose from. I particularly like *Viburnum bodnantense*, which provides pink flowers in winter, and *Viburnum tinus*, which is evergreen and has white flowers over the winter and into early spring.

The *Cornus* or dogwood, and forsythia, both popular shrubs, are good garden stalwarts. The former, which has stems of either dark red or yellow, shows up particularly well against winter snow when there is no other colour around. Forsythia is always welcome with its early show of yellow flowers and has the extra attraction of providing branches for the house when flowers are few in the garden and expensive to buy.

Buying Shrubs

The more popular shrubs sometimes derided as 'common' are usually easily and quickly propagated. This means that you can afford to stock a border fairly quickly and painlessly, leaving aside the more special and exotic shrubs. Such shrubs as *Cornus* and forsythia are often offered by market traders, bare root – that is, just as they are lifted from the earth – in the early part of the year. Although they may look like unpromising specimens, showing no leaf and appearing to be little more than a collection of stems, they can be a good buy.

Market traders who use a pitch repeatedly have a reputation to protect, and want to encourage you to make repeat purchases, so they will probably be able and willing to offer any advice you might need.

If, however, you prefer to buy plants grown in containers from a garden centre, for example, you will find the prices steeper. You may be willing to pay the extra, perhaps because you are planting shrubs out of season, but take care to get your money's worth.

A good specimen

First shop around for the best prices. Prices for identical shrubs can vary greatly and it is worth doing a comparison if you have more than one outlet in your neighbourhood. Check the plants carefully, too. Try picking up the plant by its central stem – if it lifts easily out of its pot you can assume it was not grown in the container but recently planted into it. Look at the base of the pot: if there is a mass of tangled roots growing out of the pot the plant has been in there too long and may be feeling rather starved.

A poor specimen

Consider the overall shape of the shrub for the position you have in mind, and make sure it looks healthy. Check that no creepy-crawlies have been using it to house their eggs. The soil in the container should be a good colour and weed-free: pots which are full of weed indicate a certain neglect and you don't want to introduce more or new weeds into your border.

Finally, if you find a plant you are satisfied with, buy it and make a mental note that you have found a good nursery.

Shrubs are sometimes sold in supermarkets, both bare root and in containers, perhaps more cheaply than you will see advertised by garden centres, but it pays to take care. The ideal shopping conditions for buying biscuits and jars of jam are often not the ideal conditions for keeping and displaying plants. You could find plants being forced into early growth by the warmth or drying out and dying. This need not be the case, of course but it is wise to have a close look at whatever you are tempted to buy, or your bargain could be a disappointment.

If you are lucky enough to have a local Women's Institute market in your town make a bee-line for it. Besides cakes, fresh produce and home-made goods the W.I. can be a rich source of plants and shrubs sold at very reasonable prices. Moreover as the plants have probably come from the gardens of those women selling them you will be offered all sorts of hints and tips on their cultivation.

Borders

When planning your borders don't be too regimented. Don't think in terms of straight lines and boxes of colour but aim instead for a softer approach using swirls of colour and gently sweeping bands of plants. Nothing looks more unnatural than a strictly planned and executed planting scheme where one geranium is interspersed with six lobelia plants and every two yards a fuchsia rears up. It is much easier on the eye to allow for some overlap between plants, aiming at groupings which lead the eye on to another or combinations of varieties, colour, and form.

To Summarise

The summer bedding garden, then, offers scope for gardening both on a small and large scale. It could be contained in pots or used to enhance a more permanent planting scheme. But if you don't have time to raise seeds and the yearly change-over seems like too much hard work you might prefer a more relaxed type of gardening. You might like to try the increasingly popular wild garden. This does not mean abandoning your plot to weeds and the annoyance of your neighbours, who would have to cope with floating weed seeds, but planning a more natural garden which depends on native plants for its gentle appeal.

THE WILD GARDEN

The wild garden deserves its name not only because of its appearance but because of its ability to attract wildlife. You will find that a whole host of birds, butterflies, moths, bees and other insects, and even a hedgehog if you are lucky, will visit your garden if you choose this form of planting.

The wild garden is primarily a garden in which nature is allowed to reassert itself. You will not be concerned with rigid planting systems, hand weeding, deep digging or muck spreading. But before you relax completely you will have to 'manage' the development of your garden to avoid it becoming nothing more than an unattractive tangle of weed and thistle.

Combining Styles of Garden

If you like the idea of an informal garden but are worried about keeping a seating area and play area for the children, don't be. The two are not mutually exclusive. Even in a small garden you could meet both needs by having a patio with a few well filled containers and hanging baskets for colour, surrounded by a cropped lawn which in turn is bounded by an area of much longer grass. Alternatively you could plan a conventional garden with traditional borders, but use plants which are particularly attractive to wildlife and earmark a particular corner for long grass. This can work almost anywhere but I would hesitate to recommend having the wild area next to your vegetable patch, where it is particularly important to keep weeds at bay.

Yet another possibility if you have a large garden is that of creating a garden within a garden. Use paths to demarcate the various areas and lead a path through the wild area so that you can easily enjoy the 'wilderness'. This could even be part of an energy-saving strategy for anyone trying to cut down on the demands of a large garden, as a wild garden obviously needs a good deal less tending.

Grass

Wherever you plan to site your wild area, you can choose how much effort to put into it. You could sow an area of grass and wildflowers onto bare ground if you have not yet created a lawn.

Special mixtures of wild grasses and flowers are available already made up and can be sown in April or September as for an ordinary lawn. There are mixes to suit particular soil conditions; for example you can buy packs for clay soils, chalky soils and loam.

If, however, you already have a lawn and don't want to go to the trouble of digging it all up to get at the bare earth you could simply allow the existing grass to grow. Don't mow every week but keep the area manageable with a sickle, cutting or harvesting the grass after your plants have flowered and set seed.

Wildflowers

To make the area prettier and more interesting both for yourself and wildlife you could introduce some wildflowers. Cowslips, primroses and violets are always welcome in the spring, as are clumps of daffodils allowed to naturalise amongst the grasses. Scottish bluebells, and field and Welsh poppies look at home and corn marigolds and cornflowers add extra colour in the summer.

Plants can be bought in from garden centres and transplanted into the grass, but this is obviously more expensive than raising your own from seed. If you are confining the wild garden to a very small area, however, you might find the cost small enough to justify in terms of the instant transformation.

Costs, too, can be offset in terms of multiplying the plants the next year by dividing them. Plants like primroses can be easily split up after they have finished flowering, by lifting them from the soil and using a sharp knife to divide up the plant into its various subdivisions. These divisions can be replanted to make a number of new plants, each with its own root system.

Wildflower Seed

As the wild garden is becoming more popular the choice of wildflower seed is becoming wider and more readily available. The majority of seed, being native, is not hard to grow but unfortunately some seeds, like cowslip and primrose, take a while to germinate; it may be over a year before they show much sign of life, so you do have to be patient.

Don't waste seed simply by scattering it over an already grassed area. Despite your best intentions it will not turn into a patchwork meadow of yore. You must first reveal bare earth by raking out grass and weed. Don't use any fertiliser either in hope of spurring growth, as the poorer the soil the better. If the soil is too rich, surrounding grass will tend to overrun your seed before it has a chance to develop. Make sure the seed is firmly embedded in the soil and cover it up lightly.

Alternatively you can raise your seed in trays and grow it on to a suitable stage for transplanting into the ground.

Borders

If you would rather start a wild garden by concentrating on existing borders you could think about those bushes and trees which are particularly attractive to birds, butterflies and bees. Birds enjoy the berries provided by the mountain ash tree, holly and elder bush, and they will also feed on the seeds of teasels and forget-me-not flowers. Yarrow and marjoram act as magnets to bees, and butterflies cannot resist *Sedum spectabile* with its flat densely packed fleshy flower heads, commonly known as butterfly plant. Don't neglect ivies either, as they provide an important cover for butterflies and moths, and even birds if they are dense enough.

Water Features

If you can, think about providing a water feature, as this might attract a frog or toad as well as numerous aquatic insects. If you cannot afford a pool or do not have enough space, you could contain it to an old barrel. Cut the barrel in half, line it with polythene to make it watertight and fill with water. Don't try to keep fish in it as there won't be enough room but you could introduce a miniature water lily and some water snails. Even this miniature water feature could be dangerous, however, if you have young children around, so take care in siting it to make sure they cannot accidentally topple in.

As well as thinking about the type of plants and the more relaxed form of cultivation in a wild garden, think about actively encouraging visitors with things like a bird table, bath and bat box. Itinerant hedgehogs may even repay you by eating a few slugs from the vegetable patch.

To Summarise The wild garden will introduce sound to your garden in the form of bird song and the hum of insects, it will relieve you of many of the traditional garden chores and it will look attractive, given time. It is not a garden to rush but one which will develop slowly. Even then you might have to put up with a few cheeky comments from those not in the know, and if you yourself begin to fidget at the sight of dandelions and daisies in the 'lawn', try something else.

THE COTTAGE GARDEN

My own particular favourite is the cottage garden. It is becoming increasingly popular nowadays, perhaps because of nostalgia for the 'good old days' when the pace of life was thought to be quieter, or perhaps as a backlash against the high-tech environment of many working lives. Whatever the reason, people tend to idealise the 'roses round the door' type of garden. Generally they do not have in mind a true reconstruction of an old cottage garden but rather a garden made up from herbaceous or hardy perennial plants which grow, flower, die down and repeat the cycle annually, only needing lifting after five years or so, when they benefit from being divided.

A true cottage garden was designed to meet the needs of a farm labourer and his family, supplying them with fresh vegetables, fruit, herbs and a few flowers. Every inch of available soil was cultivated, plants being given only just as much space as they needed to maximise yields. While we do not need to use our gardens for quite the same purposes, the modern cottage garden, in common with its predecessor, crams plants into every available space.

In the cottage garden you need not be overly concerned with weeding. By allowing plants to sow seed around, you will discover new and unthought-of combinations of plants springing up and, galling though it is, these combinations can be better than any planned with thoughtful study. Plants and nature seem to work together to site plants in ways which work effortlessly. This increases the sense of harmony in the garden and breaks up any possible hard lines. You can of course help nature by planting in groups of three or five. These uneven numbers of plants tend to look better and less formal than plants in twos or fours.

While tidying up is not a major chore, then, you do have to be prepared to get your soil in good heart before you start planting. You are hoping for a patchwork effect covering up

Water is a luxury in a garden but always be aware of the danger to toddlers

the earth totally, so you have to feed the soil so that it can support all this growth. Little can be done when the plants are in place so when the border is empty work in as much manure, compost or leaf mould as you can. This not only improves the soil's fertility but its drainage and appearance. Thereafter while plants are *in situ* you can only mulch around them, as to attempt to dig compost in would cause as much harm as good to the plant's root structures.

Building Materials

The cottage garden does not simply suit country cottage style housing or old terraced homes, as its gentle appeal and often blousy air when in full bloom can complement almost any type of building. Care should be taken, however, in choosing hard materials for construction in the garden. Garish colours are not suitable, nor are obviously synthetic materials. It is better to look to things like gravel or crushed bark for paths, or alternatively you could choose slabs laid into the lawn like stepping stones. Old stone and flags obviously fit in with the ambience, as do any old pieces of garden furniture in the forms of benches, tables and urns. You can also use rustic poles to effect, to make arches and pergolas over which you can train old roses, clematis or honeysuckle.

Plants

You will not suffer from lack of choice when creating a garden based on herbaceous plants. There really is a vast range from which to choose. They come in just about every colour you could possibly imagine, in differing heights and forms to suit varying conditions; they flower at different times over a long period and are generally fairly easy going, requiring little attention. And apart from these many virtues some of the traditional flowers provide the additional bonus of scent, which characterises the cottage garden.

Climbing roses can be used to climb up walls and fences or scramble over old tree stumps or sheds. They can cover arches and entrances to provide visitors with a welcoming fragrance. Rose bushes also have their place in the cottage garden, but avoid segregating them in a separate border. It is more attractive to see them growing in a sunny border, underplanted perhaps with garlic, catmint and polyanthus, violets and candytuft.

Planning Beds

Plan beds either set against fences or walls, or in 'islands' surrounded by grass or paths. Those beds which are backed by fences or walls should have the tallest growing plants at the back. This is not an iron rule, however, as although smaller plants should not be hidden by taller plants, it is interesting to occasionally put a tall plant near the front of the border so that it causes the eye to stop and study the area more carefully. The same applies to island beds, where the tall plants are usually

Chives

Some of the many varieties of herb

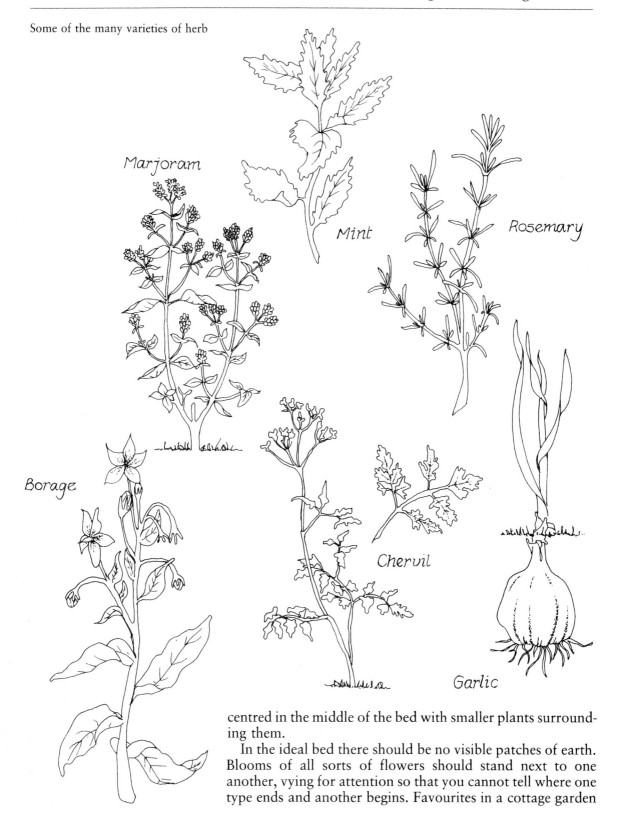

Marjoram

Mint

Rosemary

Borage

Chervil

Garlic

centred in the middle of the bed with smaller plants surrounding them.

In the ideal bed there should be no visible patches of earth. Blooms of all sorts of flowers should stand next to one another, vying for attention so that you cannot tell where one type ends and another begins. Favourites in a cottage garden are the informal type of flowers, such as delphiniums, lupins, columbine, cranesbill, and oriental poppies. Wallflowers, sweet william, foxgloves, cornflowers and pansies are all easily grown and colourful additions to the list of suitable plants.

There is also a great range of herbs from which to choose. These need not be set aside in a special part of the garden but can increase a border's appeal by being planted both in amongst it and at the front. Rosemary, lavender, mint and borage give height, marjoram and hyssop delicious flowers and chervil, garlic and chives attractive leaf form or shape.

Staking If you grow a lot of tall plants which have a floppy habit or tend to suffer from wind damage, such as delphiniums and oriental poppies, you should be prepared to stake these plants before the damage occurs. Nothing looks more ugly and untidy than groups of plants tied round with knitting wool or string and attached to a bamboo cane for support. Unfortunately this is all too often seen, spoiling the display of otherwise well designed borders. You must anticipate the likelihood of plants falling over and before they are even half way grown insert stakes for their support which are then hidden by the subsequent growth. There are many plant supports on the market but I prefer those which cost nothing: these are no more than twiggy sticks picked up from the dead undergrowth on a forest walk. They are used for a season, discarded, burnt on the fire and new ones collected the next year.

Multiplication With plants like delphinium, cranesbill, catmint and so on it is quicker to start off new plants from pieces which have been divided from a mother plant than to grow from seed. You can either buy such plants bare root or grown in pots for immediate transition to the garden or, hopefully, find yourself the recipient of them as gifts from gardening friends. This would not be sheer altruism on their part as most herbaceous plants actually benefit from being split up every so often. Plants should be divided when they get too big and start to hide their companions, or when they start to die off in the centre.

If all this sounds rather complicated and too much trouble, don't be put off. In many ways the cottage garden looks after itself. Unlike the summer bedding garden in which plants have to be lifted and removed after they have finished flowering, the cottage garden plants are left where they are to increase in size and bloom the next year. You can cut the plants back if they bloom early in the year in the hope of getting a second late flush of flowers but this is not essential. Nor is it necessary to remove top growth after flowers have past as it can help shelter the crowns of plants against the worst of winter's frosts.

Moreover, the top growth often has a beauty of its own, for example honesty can look very attractive in its winter form.

The cottage garden is very much about cycles – the continuing pattern of growth, bloom and dying back illustrated by the hardy perennial plants. It is not about formal planting patterns but is firmly bedded in a gardener's love of plants, plants and more plants. If in addition to the herbaceous plants you use fruit trees such as apple and plums, climbing plants such as wisteria and ivies and a few bushes such as the fragrant witch hazel and *Viburnum burkwoodii* you will be able to prolong interest in the garden as well as giving height and substance when the herbaceous plants are in their dormant phase.

To Summarise The cottage garden owes much of its charm to its feeling of plenty, its abundance of colour and scent. It really is a garden which you 'over tidy' at your peril. If you are tempted just to tidy up this bit or prune that rose my advice would be, don't. Leave things as they are, relax, and sit down to enjoy your garden. Nothing can be nicer than to sit in a cottage garden at the peak of its beauty, perhaps in June, on a warm evening enjoying its charm with a glass of a favourite wine in hand. So, if you can, put down the trowel and secateurs for a bit and simply experience the garden.

OTHER ALTERNATIVES

Despite the virtues of a cottage garden, some people might still not be affected by its appeal. Perhaps its blousy appearance seems twee or just too messy. There are, however, numerous other garden styles to choose from, as well as those already considered, either for a whole garden or as just a part or 'room' within a large garden. You may for instance opt for rockery gardening or even the specialist form of scree bed with tiny alpine plants. There is a whole industry devoted to servicing the needs of those who prefer water gardening, with special aquatic plants and fish. You might think conifers and heathers are the thing and wish to devote your energy to a study of those. The list of plants and their merits is endless, as are the uses and planting combinations we each favour. I have merely tried here to indicate the popular choices available either to a new gardener or one who is trying to alter an existing garden.

The types of garden described here are only representations to give a flavour of what can be achieved. Don't feel hidebound by convention. You are free to create your garden as you wish, either by promoting a style or mixing up elements from various styles to make your own concoction.

2 PLANNING FOR YOUR NEEDS

Here you are full of enthusiasm and ready to go but where do you begin? How do you convert an area of dirt and rubble into the garden of your dreams? Or perhaps the problem is an existing garden which is 'alright' but rather boring, or, even worse, designed in the worst possible taste in your opinion – someone else's garden feature being your nightmare. How do you improve matters? Don't panic and don't rush out to start digging madly. There will be time enough for all that elbow grease later. First step back and consider what you have.

Happily garden planning, although one of the most important stages in creating the ideal garden, need not cost a penny. A few sheets of paper, a pen and some imagination are all you need to get started and the effort expended now will repay itself numerous times over in terms of satisfaction in a well-arranged garden.

If you have a brand new home and garden you may think you have nothing but a dirt-enclosed rectangle, but look at it another way: if you have weeds the soil is capable of supporting other more pleasing growth, and you have the most desirable commodity of all – freedom. You have a blank space which you can mould as you will, without fear of being compromised by anyone else's ideas.

If you are planning to redesign an existing garden which is new to you, wait and see what the seasons bring. A corner of the garden which looks extremely dull at the moment may burst into life in the spring with unsuspected bulbs and plants such as hosta, which give no hint of their existence in winter. It is a shame to lose plants simply through ignorance of their existence.

PRIORITIES IN PLANNING

When planning your dream garden think primarily of who will use it. If you have children you will probably want to encourage them to play in the garden, rather than out on the pavement. Unfortunately this does not simply entail erecting a swing in the garden, and expecting them to get on with it. If you are too fussy with your borders or object to children playing ball on the grass as it ruins your lawn, you could be heading for problems.

You can tackle such problems, which basically stem from differing priorities, in a number of ways. You could, for

The segregated garden

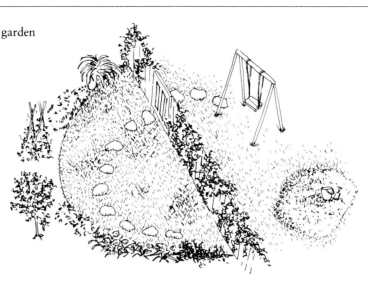

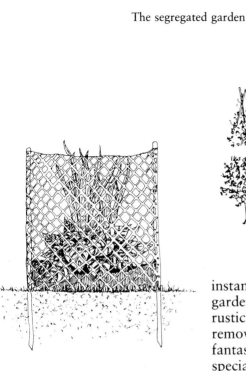

instance, segregate the children to a particular part of the garden, even going so far as to mark it off with trellis fencing or rustic poles. Plants could be further protected by screens of removable wire netting. This would leave you free to indulge fantasies of a billiard table-like lawn surrounded with specialist plants.

However, I am a little sceptical about this essentially defensive approach to gardening. Young children cannot be left alone even in the comparative safety of their own garden. Even a non-poisonous plant or berry could result in a nasty tummy ache if consumed in quantity by a voracious toddler. And children seem to have an uncanny knack of hurting themselves on the most innocuous of toys as soon as you turn your back. Besides, if your children are anything like mine, they will refuse to be left on their own and are only happy if allowed to 'work' alongside or at least feel they can have your full attention when necessary. I believe you are best to abandon ideas of an exquisitely perfect garden until children are old enough to appreciate the need for care themselves. Much better to plan your garden positively with children very much in mind. This way you can all enjoy the extension of the family home and hopefully nurture a love together of planting and growing things.

Security Measures
Fishponds

Where children are around the first priority must be to re-design any obviously dangerous features. Fill in, drain or securely cover any fishpond. If you cover it, and this applies to wells too, make sure the cover cannot be removed by prying fingers and that it is strong enough to support any child who may be tempted to crawl over or lie on it. The best answer perhaps, is, to fill the pond in altogether so you no longer need worry. This is not necessarily irreversible. You can always uncover or excavate it later on, but for the moment how about converting it into a sandpit?

All you need do is fill the bottom with some rubble for drainage, top with pea gravel, firm it into place and cover the lot with an eight inch layer of sand. Use special river-washed sand, as ordinary builder's sand, although great for making sand castles, stains clothing. You may wish to construct some sort of cover which will keep animals off when the pit is not being used – chicken wire will serve this purpose, or a more deluxe cover can be made from scrap wood, treated with preservative if you are concerned to keep the weather out.

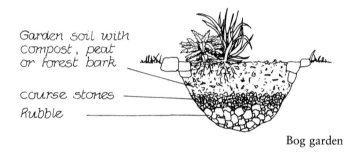

Garden soil with compost, peat or forest bark

coarse stones

Rubble

Bog garden

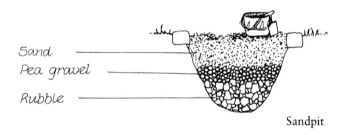

Sand

Pea gravel

Rubble

Sandpit

If you can't face the thought of a sandpit or the pool is in an inconvenient or shady position, how about turning it into a bog plant area? To do this, fill the bottom area with rubble topped with coarse stones to a level of about twelve inches. On top of this add your garden soil mixed with compost, peat or forest bark. You now have an area which, because of the pond lining, will be more water-retentive than other parts of the garden. In the summer, if it shows any sign of drying out, it is an easy matter to play the hose on it for an hour or so.

You can plant the area up with a selection of plants unique to this type of environment, anything from water iris to ferns, or primulas and monkey musk. You will be able to enjoy a whole variety of plants which might not survive elsewhere in your garden and if you are short of ideas you can always consult plant and seed catalogues, which are usually supplied free of charge by mail order from a number of well-known horticultural companies.

Running Water Running water is another potential danger as it is always attractive to children. Where this takes the form of a stream running through or at the bottom of your garden, make sure children cannot have access to it. Very steep slopes or flights of steps are hazardous too, so make sure children cannot topple over accidentally, by providing adequate handrails or barriers.

Poisonous Plants In established gardens, obvious dangers can come from the plants themselves. If you are in any doubt about which are poisonous, consult a text book. Your Health Visitor may even be able to provide a leaflet showing the more commonly planted poisonous varieties such as laburnum, yew, lupins and foxglove. If your children are not yet old enough to understand the dangers it may be best to remove them from the garden altogether, I mean the plants of course!

Chemicals Don't leave poisonous chemicals such as pesticides, insecticides, slug pellets or petrol around for curious fingers and mouths to find. Make sure that if you plan to use such chemicals you have a safe store for them, preferably not in the house and certainly well out of the reach of children.

Glass Finally if you inherit an old greenhouse or cold frame which has broken glass panes, make it a priority to repair or demolish it before anyone can hurt themself.

DESIGNING GARDENS
WITH CHILDREN IN MIND

Looking at the positive aspect of garden design, wherever possible plan things to please; remember children love to make dens in 'secret' places. You might consider leaving part of your garden in a semi-wild state to add to the mystery of such games. I don't simply mean letting weeds take over a corner of the garden, nor do I see it as a purely selfless act. By simply allowing the grass to grow under apple trees and planting a few wild flowers you will enjoy the bonus of increasing the amount of wildlife to visit your garden. I know this probably won't do your apples a great deal of good and all the standard text books tell you to remove grass from the base of fruit trees to increase yield, but happily gardening is all about compromise and doing whatever suits your needs best, so don't feel guilty about not following received wisdom to the letter.

Children also appreciate having an area of cropped grass to play games on – anything from badminton to croquet, golf and football. All games, even played on a small scale, take up a considerable amount of room and are hard on grass. Bear in mind when you plan the size and type of a new lawn, games will be cramped and a source of frustration if you make it too small. If you choose the wrong sort of turf or grass seed you could also end up making an expensive mistake. You can actually buy seed especially designed for family wear which provides a hard-wearing lawn, as opposed to the finer growth prized by gardeners who wish to achieve a perfect green sward as a foil to plants.

Outdoor Toys

Because there is a great deal of activity around outdoor toys such as swings, climbing frames and trampolines they take a heavy toll on grass. But don't be tempted to place any sort of activity equipment on a hard surface. Children can and do fall off such equipment with alarming regularity and they will obviously hurt themselves much more falling onto unyielding concrete rather than grass. If you are particularly concerned to prevent wear and tear on your lawn you could invest in a special mesh product which you place directly onto the grass and over which you can mow as the grass grows through it. This, it is claimed, takes the brunt of the damage without being unpleasing to the eye.

A Child's Own Patch

It is fun to incorporate into the garden a special area solely for children to cultivate. Obviously it has to be a relatively small patch so that they do not tire of the work involved before seeing any results. It could be a corner of vegetable ground, a piece of flower border or even just a container or window box. Wherever you can find room for your child's special garden, take care to clearly demarcate it. This can be fairly simply achieved by bricks, railway sleepers or rustic poles, anything in fact, just so long as the child can easily recognise his own patch.

Children are usually thrilled to see the result of their labours, no matter how straggly or weedy looking, but they do like to have plants which grow quickly. Try the easiest, almost foolproof seeds to start with, perhaps radishes or a couple of potatoes in the vegetable area, or some cornflowers or sunflowers in the border. In a container you could try candytuft or nasturtiums. All these seeds can be sown directly into the soil outside and need no special care. If you make sure they are watered if in danger of drying out and not actually sown into rock hard soil all should be well. You might even find your children develop a love of gardening and green fingers to rival your own.

Raised Beds

If anyone in your family is confined to a wheelchair or simply has trouble bending it is worth considering including a few raised beds in the scheme of things. Constructed at a suitable

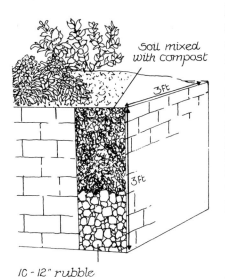

Soil mixed with compost

3 ft

3 ft

10 - 12" rubble

Raised beds are useful for those who have difficulty bending

height such beds can easily be looked after and enjoyed from a sitting position. They are easily constructed from brick or even old railway sleepers. Make a rectangular box up to about six feet across if you can tend it from both sides, otherwise make it only three foot across. Fill with about ten to twelve inches of rubble for drainage and then top with soil mixed with compost to a height of about two feet. You could even use such beds to grow a variety of plants not normally suited to your garden, perhaps those which require greater drainage than found in the garden as a whole. However you choose to plant raised beds, they look particularly attractive sited round a patio, where they make a good divide between the hard texture of the patio and the rest of the garden.

PETS

Pets are yet another consideration when planning your plot, as their needs can impinge on your ideas. Most of the smaller varieties such as guinea pigs and rabbits are easily taken care of by a hutch and run which can be moved around the garden.

Dogs are a bigger consideration but need not be a deterrent to the keen gardener. It is worth starting from the first day to teach it to toilet in a specially selected area. This means you won't have to be constantly clearing up after the beast and children will not face any danger of falling into faeces. Dogs can be taught to keep off borders if you correct them every time they stray from the grass, but if your four legged friend is as stupid as my spaniel you will realise this is an uphill task. Remember too the dangers of using slug pellets and certain weed-killers when animals are around. Always read product labels and keep animals out of the garden if they are likely to be in any danger.

Finally, if you or your neighbours own a cat and you want to be especially kind you can always plant a patch of catmint for the animal to thrash around in. If however the cat is one of those beasts which insists on digging holes in the soil, although there are various repellants on the market, perhaps all you can do is tactfully ignore it.

PATIOS

Think carefully about where you intend to site a patio. Most people tack them onto their houses outside their sitting room window, but first consider the setting of your home. There is little point putting a patio outside a north facing window which gets little or no sun after early morning. Nor is there much point in having a patio which is directly overlooked, as you will regret the loss of privacy. Take time to study the angles of your garden: find out how the sun hits it and where the most sheltered areas are. You might find the best place is outside your kitchen door, or some distance from your house at the bottom of the garden.

A patio need not be a simple rectangle of paving slabs laid one in front of another; consider a half-moon shape which might echo bow windows, or think about laying paving on an angle to make a different pattern. There are many possible options and now is the time to consider which you would prefer. Companies supplying slabs and building stone often provide leaflets showing different ways of using their goods and you might get some new ideas from these, even if you intend to construct your patio from a different material. At the same time you might also plan a permanent barbeque. A three-sided rectangular brick box can be simply erected to house a free standing barbeque. This ensures it cannot be accidentally toppled over and is free from gusts of wind.

Whatever style you decide on and however you construct your patio, make sure that it will be big enough to accommodate your needs. Make space not only for a table and chairs, but for people moving around and children playing. Think big rather than small as it is only too easy to underestimate the size.

Think about patio styles

PATHS

Ideally garden paths should be wide enough for two people to walk abreast, and you should make them even wider if anyone in your family uses a wheelchair. Paths can be completely hard, made from materials such as concrete or stone, or you could investigate the possibility of using gravel or forest bark or simply sunken paving stones in grass.

BUILDING MATERIALS

Even at this early stage it is worth deciding on the type of materials to be used for building in the garden. The choice of hard materials is vast, including various sizes of gravel and grit, old bricks, granite cobbles, concrete slabs, stone and reconstituted stone and broken paving. Local authorities often sell broken slabs very cheaply, from two to three pounds a ton, which is ideal for crazy paving. If you are on a very tight budget such paving, although labour intensive, is ideal for constructing patios and garden paths.

If you long to use natural stone in the garden but fear the cost is prohibitive you might like to try approaching any firm which is carrying out large scale building in your locale. In digging out foundations they may discover unwanted stone which they are willing to part with cheaply or even freely. If you do come by such stone wait and see how it performs during a hard frost before undertaking any major construction. You may be unfortunate and find the stone is too soft to withstand a penetrating frost and simply disintegrates. This is disappointing but not as frustrating as watching a carefully constructed wall crumble before your eyes.

Whatever type of material you choose to use, and your choice will naturally be affected by your budget, try to ensure that it complements your home. Nothing looks worse say, than a lengthy concrete path tacked on to the back of a Victorian brick-built cottage; much better to choose gravel, which would probably be as cheap to install.

POSITIONING ESSENTIAL GARDEN EQUIPMENT

At the same time as thinking about patios and paths, consider the other practicalities of life, namely where you are going to put the rubbish bin, coal bunker, woodshed and compost heap. All these things should be fairly near your back door so you have easy access to them. Make sure there is a hard path to the area, as in the autumn and winter, grass will often be wet and muddy. As such essentials are unlikely to be aesthetically pleasing in themselves it is as well to think from the beginning of ways of disguising them, perhaps behind a trellis, up which you can train fast growing climbers, or simply with a piece of panelled fencing.

The Washing Line

The washing line or rotary clothes drier is often a difficult item to position. You want it to be in an airy spot, where it will not become entangled with shrubs or trees, close to the house but not an eyesore. A washing line takes up more room when clothes are drying but disappears from sight when not in use. You can even go so far as to disguise the support pole with a pillar rose. The rotary drier is more compact but less easy to make unobtrusive. Perhaps the best idea is to compromise, using a rotary drier but removing it completely from its holder for storage in the garage on days when you want the garden to look especially good.

The Greenhouse

There are numerous types of greenhouse to choose from and even if you hope to buy second hand it is worth visiting a large garden centre to get some idea of the different types around. Some are glazed with glass, others with a strong plastic, some are free standing, others are lean-tos which tack onto the side of your house or garage, some are timber framed, others have supports made from aluminium. There are various sizes and shapes to choose from, too. Apart from the well-known rectangular model you can now buy hexagons, rounds and ones with fancy arches. If you can afford to spend quite a bit of money you will be able to buy something which is a real asset to your garden in terms of looks as well as work space. But even if your means are more modest try to go for as large a greenhouse as you can as it is amazing how quickly you can occupy the space.

Whatever you choose, the siting of a greenhouse is all important. It needs to be a good clear level site, out of the way of over-hanging branches and falling leaves. The nearer it is to the house the cheaper it will be to install water and electricity, if you so choose. It is useful too to have a decent path to the greenhouse as you will probably use it when bad weather stops you getting out in the rest of the garden, and it is pleasant to be able to make trips outside without fear of muddy shoes.

Greenhouse gardening is a whole 'specialist' sub-culture of gardening with a wealth of commodities accompanying it. However, having sited the greenhouse suitably, all you really need to begin is a slipproof path through the house and some basic form of shelving to support your plants and trays. You will probably find that staging along one side of the house is quite sufficient as you can then use the full height of the house to grow tomatoes on the other side.

As with all gardening, don't be tempted into making impulsive buys for the greenhouse. Wait until you know exactly what you want and need.

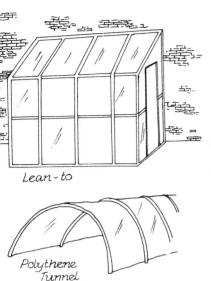

Lean-to

Polythene Tunnel

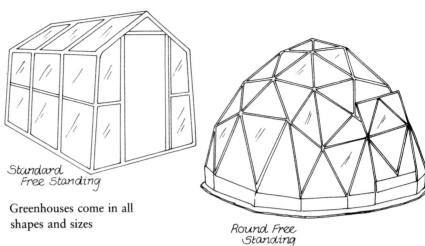

Standard Free Standing

Greenhouses come in all shapes and sizes

Round Free Standing

To Summarise   When planning the design of your garden first think about your basic needs. Take into account who, apart from yourself, will be in the garden: your children, your parents perhaps, your pets, and how they will use the area. Consider too where to site a sitting area, where paths should be laid and how any possible eyesores such as a coal or wood store or rubbish bin should be screened.

You may find it useful to draw up a couple of lists of things which can be done immediately such as removing any dangerous features, and tasks which may involve spending a bit of money such as building the patio. It is sometimes handy too, to rough out an outline sketch of the garden to help you envisage where paths will go and where you propose to put the clothes drier.

If you can, it will help you if you draw out a scale plan. Graph paper is helpful when doing this. If you feel this beyond you or too fiddly try to jot down as many of your ideas as possible in words. Make lists of plants, their positions and combinations and if possible make rough free hand sketches. No-one else need see them, so don't be discouraged if, like me, you'll never make an artist. These plans are useful to refer to when you actually get out in the garden and are digging it over. It is certainly easier to correct mistakes on paper than it is in reality. It might save you a lot of time and effort if for example you realise at this stage that the rose you are planning will obstruct your clothes drier. It is amazing how easily you can get carried away and overlook obvious follies in your eagerness to get on when you have a spade in your hand.

3 ESSENTIAL GARDENING EQUIPMENT

Before you can tackle any work in the garden you obviously need some basic tools. Little can be done by enthusiasm alone. There is, however, an almost bewildering array of machinery and gadgetry on the market. A whole industry has built up around the amateur gardener. It is now possible to purchase anything from a fancy machine to collect leaves from a lawn to a pair of spikey soles which slip over your shoes to pierce and aerate the grass; never mind that they resemble something a Roman gladiator might wear.

It is easy to be tempted into making the wrong purchase when faced with a wonderful display of hardware, especially if you don't know what you really want or need. You may already have a few tools which you wish to supplement or you may be starting from scratch, either way it is essential to sort out priorities and make a list.

TOOLS FOR DIGGING

My first choice would be the best **spade** I could afford. A spade is one of the most used tools in the garden. It can be used to chop turf, dig holes, turn over soil, mix compost or cement, lift paving stones and cut off stubborn roots, so it is worth taking trouble to find one which suits you personally. You can even buy specially adapted spades which work on a leverage system and are particularly useful for those with bad backs who cannot afford to do too much bending.

I prefer a small or border spade as I can handle it easily and don't get too tired working over a large area. However, whichever form you choose, and they vary in price from just a few pounds to well into double figures for the best in stainless steel, have a good look at what's available. Test for weight and the feel in your hands. As with all tools, make sure the handle is smooth and comfortable to hold, and the neck of the spade fits well onto the shaft.

Although you will probably be able to buy a secondhand spade, I think the amount of work you can expect from a spade means that you should treat yourself to a new one. Treated properly, which simply entails cleaning off excess muck after use and wiping the blade over with an oiled rag, a good spade should last as long as you.

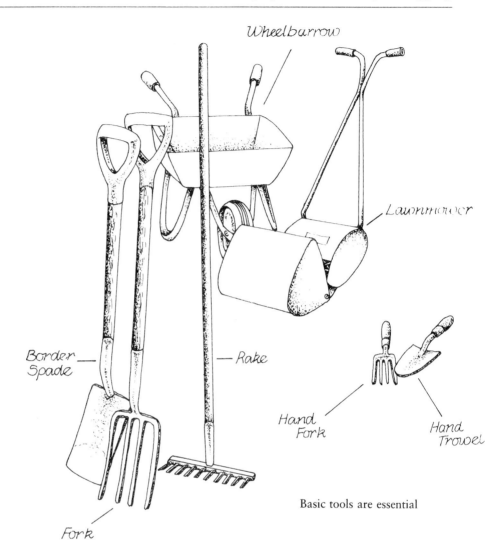

Wheelbarrow

Lawnmower

Border
Spade

Rake

Hand
Fork

Hand
Trowel

Fork

Basic tools are essential

A **fork** is another essential in the garden toolkit. It has a number of uses including spreading mulches over the borders, breaking up clods of earth, loading the compost heap, gathering up piles of twiggy growth, mixing compost and lifting potatoes from the soil. It is also a valuable tool for aerating the grass. By going over the lawn with a fork piercing the grass at regular intervals you can encourage drainage and help revitalise tired grass.

TOOLS FOR WEEDING

You will also appreciate having a **hand trowel** and **hand fork** for close work in the borders. Once a few plants are established it is all too easy to disturb and break roots when working round about them with long-handled tools. I find weeding with a hand fork by far the most satisfactory and tidy way of cleaning up a border. You can make sure you get the roots of the little devils out, and remove them from the surface of the soil for disposal elsewhere.

A hand trowel makes light work of putting in small plants and bulbs where the more cumbersome spade would struggle. It is also very useful when tending plant containers, particularly if they are made from a breakable material such as terracotta or porcelain, which cracks if treated too harshly.

Make sure that both trowel and fork are strongly made, as a heavy soil will soon bend and snap the head off a tool which is too flimsily constructed. If you do decide to buy hand tools it is a good idea to paint the handles with a bright colour – whatever you have left over from decorating will do. This way you are less likely to lose them if they are laid down in the border. I've spent many an infuriating half hour looking for mine after being disturbed at work.

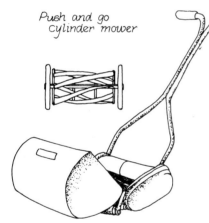

Push and go cylinder mower

TOOLS FOR MOWING

Once a lawn is established the next necessity becomes a **lawnmower**. This may well be the most costly piece of garden machinery you have to invest in, so it is worth taking time to consult various dealers to find out what is available. Do you want a powered mower? Should it be electric or petrol, and would you prefer cylinder or rotary?

Consider the area of grass to be cut and your attitude to grass-cutting first of all. Do you see it as a boring weekly chore? If you do, you will probably want a mower which cuts with the minimum of effort on your part and so would do well to opt for a powered mower. However, if you enjoy grass cutting, and apparently large numbers of people do, seeing it as a form of stress-relieving exercise, perhaps you could manage with a 'push and go' type of cylinder mower. Do be realistic, however, even if this type of mower appeals to you, it will be of no use if you have too large an area of grass to cut, or the ground is too rough. If you have to devote every spare minute to grass cutting it will almost certainly become a dreaded and unpleasant chore, making you long for the sight of smooth black tarmac which needs no maintenance. However if you are not put off by the effort involved with the 'push and go' mower, try to buy one with a roller at the back, as this allows cutting right to the edges of the lawn.

Cylinder mowers are obviously available in powered models, as are hover and rotary types, and you basically have the choice between electric and petrol power. Battery powered mowers are available but they are less common and must be

Rotary mower

Petrol mower

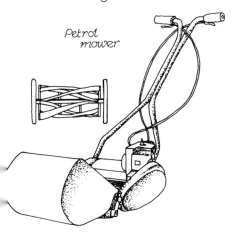

Electric mower

recharged from the mains electricity supply at regular intervals.

Any electrical tool needs care in operation and this is particularly true of mowers. If insufficient care is taken, it is all too easy to run over a live flex. Special cut-out devices which prevent the possibility of electrocution are wise investments. Always ensure you carry the cable out of the path of the mower by feeding it from behind and over your shoulder.

Electricity is of necessity limited by available power points as well as the length of cable. It can be infuriating if you have a large area of grass to cut and have to move the plug around several power points in the course of one cut. Balanced against this disadvantage, however, is the ease with which electric mowers start and operate.

Older petrol mowers can be rather difficult and fiddly to start until you get the hang of it. They can also be noisy and 'headstrong' until you get used to controlling the throttle. I can believe the stories of such mowers destroying garden fencing after being dragged around my own garden by a petrol mower in full flight with throttle jammed open. Definitely not for those of a nervous disposition.

Having decided on the type of power you would prefer, you are faced with even more options, as apart from the cylinder mower there are hovers and rotaries to choose from.

Unlike the cylinder mower, which cuts by means of a scissor action, the rotary mower has one or two spinning cutting blades supported on wheels and is particularly good over rough grass where a cylinder mower could not cope. Recent rotary models have a special type of 'blade' actually made of strong plastic which ensures you cannot chop off your toes should you accidentally run over your foot. Although it is likely still to give you bad bruising, this development is good news on the safety front.

The hover mower is similar in principle to the rotary, but instead of being supported by wheels it floats on a cushion of air. This makes it ideal for cutting slopes and banks in the garden. If you have hard edgings to your lawn you will also be able to cut right over the edge, eliminating the time-consuming job of going round with the edging shears. The hover also enables you to cut grass whilst it is still damp without turning your lawn into a mud bath – a positive advantage where the soil is heavy with clay and takes a long time to dry out.

Finally there has been a long running dispute over whether or not it is necessary to collect grass cuttings after mowing. Some argue they form a useful mulch if left lying, as they nourish the lawn. Others say you are simply spreading the weeds around and all clippings should be collected for the compost heap. Undoubtedly the lawn looks tidier if the clippings are collected and if this is important to you, go for a mower with grassbox, otherwise you will give yourself a lot of work in raking up the clippings. However if you don't think it is necessary, why bother? It's your garden, after all, and the idea is to enjoy it, not become a slave to it.

Whatever you choose, try to get the most out of your money. Rather than buy the cheapest and smallest new mower available, which could be short lived and unequal to the weekly task, if you have a large lawn to cut, go for an older, better quality secondhand model.

Caring for your Mower

After purchasing a mower don't just use it and then forget about it. It pays to clean the blades after each cut. A wire brush will remove any stubborn grass build-up and an oiled rag passed over the moving parts will help prolong life. An annual winter service prior to the first spring cut also helps to keep the motor in good working order. You really feel helpless if your mower breaks down in the middle of the growing season and you have to wait a fortnight to get it back from the repair shop, by which time your grass is approaching knee level.

TOOLS FOR WATERING

Next on my list of priorities would be a **hose**. During the first season in a new garden, when many shrubs and trees are likely to be planted, watering is extremely important. I'm sure more plants are lost by being starved of water when first put into the ground than for any other reason. It is not enough to wander round the garden giving plants a gentle spray from a watering can, like a latter day Lady Bountiful. You could in fact be doing more harm than good, by tempting fine roots to the surface where they gather the inadequate water supply and are dried out by the sun, hastening the plant's death. You need a hose to ensure an adequate water supply.

There are numerous watering systems on the market, from extremely sophisticated punctured hose types which are permanently draped around the base of plants, through the varied forms of sprinklers, to cassette packaged hoses and the straightforward hard plastic hose which comes without any storage reel.

If you want to save money, the cheapest hard type of hose attached to the kitchen tap by means of a butterfly clip can be perfectly satisfactory. If you want to leave the hose playing on a particular plant or area of the garden there are many stakes and gadgets available which secure the hose in position. But a little imagination will often achieve the same effect for nothing. I often thread the nozzle of the hose through the handle of a half-filled watering can, which is then heavy enough to hold whatever position it's put in. I have even pressed my

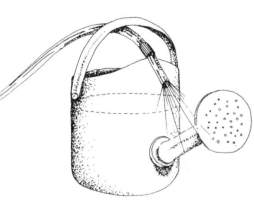

An aid to easy watering

toddler daughter's Noddy-type car into service. This proved very useful, as the hose, threaded through the car's steering wheel, could be easily manoeuvered into position, with the extra advantage that the whole thing was on wheels. However my daughter understandably got rather fed up with this imposition on her toy and demanded the car back.

After use the hard type of hose can be rather unwieldy and untidy if just left lying around the garage. It is also liable to develop kinks. It can be stored fairly easily, however, if you nail an old car wheel to the garage wall and wrap the hose around it. On the other hand, the newer flat type of hose stored on a reel, from which it is not necessary to unravel its full length before use is undoubtedly an attractive arrangement and you may wish to invest in this kind instead.

An **outside tap** is a good idea and there is a product on the market which allows you to construct an external tap yourself by tapping through an external wall to an internal cold water pipe. Perhaps you might like to suggest this sort of thing as a Christmas present.

THE WHEELBARROW

Unless you have a really tiny garden where you can carry everything by hand you will also need a wheelbarrow. Mine has survived a multitude of indignities – from barrowing children around the garden for fun, to being used as a receptacle for mixing cement. There are a number of types to choose from: double wheeled varieties, those with a large ball-like front wheel, and the traditional single narrow-wheeled type. Those with ball-type wheels are particularly useful over soft ground as they are less likely to sink in. However if you suspect any barrow is likely to compact the surface of the soil, put down wooden walk boards. The boards can be any old pieces of scrap timber provided they are wide enough to walk over.

I have found the basic traditional model of wheelbarrow very satisfactory as long as it is not overloaded. Barrows are relatively cheap to buy and can often be come by secondhand, so I think it a false economy to try to manage without one. You could be giving yourself a lot of unnecessary work. To prolong the life of a barrow always store it upended, resting against a wall or fence.

MISCELLANEOUS TOOLS

Secateurs Coming to the end of my list of essential garden tools, I would include a good pair of secateurs. You will find innumerable uses for these even if you think nothing in your garden needs trimming. They are useful when planting roses, or any other bare rooted shrub or tree, for trimming back unnecessarily long roots. Don't worry that you will be cutting off the plant's lifeline, as the water is largely carried by the thin matted-looking roots not the thick stubby variety. You also need a clean sharp cut when pruning or trimming back plants. If you leave an untidy ragged edge after hacking at a plant with scissors or the like, you not only leave the bush looking untidy but risk infecting the plant through a bruised cut.

Professional gardeners may shudder at this confession but I also use my secateurs for snipping away odd pieces of garden twine when tying up garden climbers, and opening those tough plastic bags of peat and potting compost. Sacrilege I know, but the blades seem to withstand such ill treatment.

Secateurs come in all shapes and prices; in some the blades operate in a scissor fashion and in others the blade cuts against or onto an anvil. Many are sold in boxed presentation cases and it is worth asking if you can hold them in your hand to see if they 'fit'. After all, if you plan to spend quite a bit of money on them, you want to know that they feel comfortable, are easy to operate and aren't too heavy.

It is worth mentioning here that it is useful to rub a cloth previously soaked in disinfectant over the blades of the secateurs to keep them really clean, if you are doing a lot of pruning work.

Lawn Edgers To complete the job of grass cutting you will probably need a pair of lawn edgers. These give a really neat and tidy look to a lawn. You may be able to manage with a pair of shears if your lawn is small and you are fit and active enough for all the bending; otherwise a pair of long-handled edgers are the answer. It is also possible to buy electric edging tools, which take a lot of the work out of the job, but these are far from essential.

Brush You will also need a good stiff brush to clear up the lawn clippings and do general tidying, but fortunately this is cheap to buy and should last a lifetime.

OTHER ESSENTIAL EQUIPMENT

Finally I would suggest a few items for the 'essentials' list not normally thought of as tools, namely cardboard boxes, black plastic bags, and an old set of clothes and strong heavy boots or shoes.

Clothes The clothes and boots speak for themselves. It might seem obvious but you will spend an awful lot of money on soap powder and shoe polish if you consistently dash out into the garden wearing whatever you happen to stand up in. It is almost written on tablets of stone that a quick snip over the sweet peas to remove dead heads will lead you on to noticing that new clump of weeds, and before you know where you are, you are standing spade in hand with dirt-encrusted shoes and smeared jumper.

It is important from the safety angle to wear 'sensible' gardening gear. You don't want any flapping clothing near powered machinery where it may become caught and entangled, nor do you want to be wearing open-toed sandals when mowing. Despite the all too obvious dangers, scores of people are injured in this way every summer. Even when not using powered tools it is easy to damage your feet if your concentration wavers, and you are not wearing stout footwear.

One year I had so much digging to do I managed to wear out a pair of wooden-soled clogs because of the pressure on the arch of my foot while pressing down on the spade. It seems unbelievable but shows the force involved when digging. So think twice about the chores to be done and keep a special set of gardening togs handy. Don't forget a stout pair of gloves either: those with cotton backs and hide palms are cheap to buy, flexible and strong enough to protect your hands from thorns and nettles.

Bags and Boxes Cardboard boxes come free from any friendly grocery shop and if you are lucky your local rubbish collector may be able to leave you an extra plastic bag. You will find both invaluable. The boxes are useful for collecting those weeds which are so persistent they need to be burnt or taken to a Council refuse tip, and for storing all sorts of gardening materials from plant

The ever-useful black plastic bag

pots to bulbs and potato tubers. The plastic bags can be used to start compost, either if you haven't room for a decent heap or if you just haven't had enough time to organise a proper container. Pierce the bags with a fork to let air in, and fill with a variety of garden refuse, lawn cuttings, kitchen waste and compost activator. Store on one side and by the end of the summer season you should have bags of friable compost.

The same bags split open to provide a length of plastic are also useful, pegged straight down onto the soil to give you an early start with spring planting. The plastic allows the earth to heat up a little and of course keeps it much drier and easier to work than surrounding soil.

The Compost Bin

Warming the soil

A compost bin is a great boon. Although plastic bags can be used to store garden refuse while it undergoes the magical metamorphosis into compost, if you become a keen composter, and it is something of a bug, you will soon be thinking on a grander scale.

Compost can be collected into heaps in any odd corner of the garden but at best the heaps are unsightly and at worst a real mess as they tend to sprawl over quite an area. If possible it is better either to buy a ready-made bin or container or make your own. You will find that if the compost is contained and preferably covered in some way whilst allowing air to circulate, the decomposition process will be considerably speeded up. There is a wide choice of bins on the market made in wood, plastic and metal. The price obviously varies a great deal, but don't opt for the smallest just because it is the cheapest, as you will probably find it inadequate for your needs. Compost is bulky and it doesn't take long to fill up a small bin. Try to go for one which allows you to empty compost from the bottom, otherwise you will end up in all sorts of difficulty.

If you can't justify the cost of buying a bin, why not make one? It is really very simple to construct, being basically a chicken wire box strengthened at the four corners with wooden stakes. Plan to make your box about four foot across by about eight foot long and of a height you can easily manage to load. Treat your posts with a non-plant-poisonous wood preserver and drive them into the ground at suitable intervals. Stretch the wire around three sides and staple in place. The fourth side should be removable to allow you to remove the compost as it rots down. Construct a wooden frame from scrap wood, which will fit snugly inside one side of your box. Cover this in chicken wire and slot it into place to form the last side.

Before starting to fill your container with garden refuse put down a layer of twiggy branches. This will allow air to reach the compost and stop it turning into something soggy and nasty.

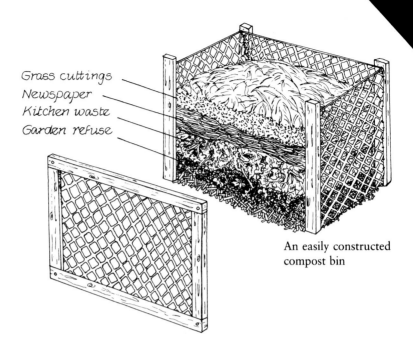

Grass cuttings
Newspaper
Kitchen waste
Garden refuse

An easily constructed
compost bin

Compost   You are now ready to begin your heap. Almost anything can
be used to get your compost going, but the key is variety. You
cannot simply tip a heap of grass cuttings in and expect it to
become glorious friable compost in a few months. Use layers
of grass cuttings, strips of damp torn up newspaper, dust from
the vacuum cleaner, the soot any friendly chimney sweep
might leave, all forms of uncooked kitchen vegetable waste,

A compost heap

crushed eggshells and other garden refuse. Some people even advocate putting urine on the heap, but personally I think rushing out to empty the potty in the garden is going a bit too far!

A little common sense will tell you that you can use practically everything from the garden, apart from plants which might have been sprayed with a poisonous weedkiller, plants which are too tough and stemmy to break down, and those weeds which are so pernicious that you are simply asking for trouble if you dispose of them in this way. Keep the heap covered with an old piece of carpet, sacking or pierced plastic sheet to keep the heat in. Remember to water the compost, particularly in hot weather, to stop it drying out and thus preventing decomposition taking place. You can buy proprietary compost activators to speed up the process of decay but layers of well-rotted farmyard manure incorporated into the heap will do the same job.

You might even find the squirrel instinct of saving all scraps, down to the tea leaves, becomes so strong you will have to make two containers to keep all your compost in. This is quite a good idea, as even well-constructed compost heaps take a while to decompose – about six months – although this should be shortened a little over the summer months when the weather is warmer.

If as you remove compost from the bottom of the heap you find bits which have not rotted down completely, you can simply put them back into the container again. If the stems look too woody, however, discard them, as they will never decompose properly and won't improve the compost.

Successful compost is dark brown and crumbly – just the stuff to mulch round plants in the borders where it will do the double job of conditioning the soil and preventing plants drying out too quickly. You have the further bonus of it making the surface of the soil look more attractive too. You can also use compost as a general soil enricher by digging it in before any planting. It really is like getting something for nothing, especially if you consider the cost of buying products which would do a similar job.

USEFUL EXTRAS

A **watering can** is a handy addition to the garden hose. Fitted with a fine rose you can water seed trays without the soil becoming compacted; without the rose the can is useful for watering containers and hanging baskets in the summer when watering could be necessary every day.

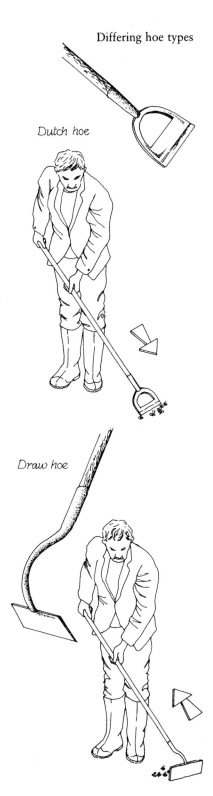

Differing hoe types

Dutch hoe

Draw hoe

Cans are made in plastic and galvanised metal. It is a matter of choice which you prefer, as the metal can be repaired if it springs a leak, whereas the plastic is lighter and won't leak, but if punctured must be thrown away.

Do be careful if you plan to mix weedkiller in your can. If possible have a separate can clearly marked and kept strictly for that purpose: if not, be sure to clean and rinse the can thoroughly after using weedkilling or insecticidal preparations to ensure you don't harm any plants by mistake.

A pleasant garden extra is a **water butt.** You can collect rainwater which is then useful for watering more temperamental species such as camellias and rhododendrons and other plants which hate the lime sometimes found in tap water. Butts can often be obtained fairly cheaply from the most unusual sources. If you watch the classified advertisements in your local paper you might see old orange juice containers being sold for this purpose.

A **rake** and **hoe** are particularly useful tools in the vegetable patch. The rake, moved back and forwards over previously broken and forked earth, helps to level and fine down the surface of the soil prior to planting. You do need a fairly large clear area of ground, however, to use a rake satisfactorily, otherwise you can easily catch low branches or surface roots of close-growing plants.

There are many different kinds of hoe available. One of the most common is the Dutch hoe, the head of which looks something like an upside-down horse shoe with a bar of metal across the bottom. It is used to remove weeds from just below the surface of the earth and to break up earth which has become lightly caked, perhaps after being quickly dried out after rain.

Another popular hoe is the draw hoe, which looks completely different from the Dutch. It has a head like a miniature inverted spade, used to draw weeds and earth towards you, and is particularly useful for earthing up vegetables like potatoes.

Of course both hoes simply leave weeds on the surface of the soil and if there is much rain, you may have to go over your work again, picking up such weeds, to prevent them rerooting in the damp conditions.

Another common tool is the **spring rake.** It bears little relation to the one used on the vegetable patch. The head is made either from thin metal or plastic spikes arranged in a fan shape. It is a fairly useful, if seasonal, tool, being basically used in the autumn to gather fallen leaves and to scarify the lawn by raking up dead and matted grass and moss.

A **half moon edger** is a useful lawn tool for ensuring a tidy and neat finish to the grass. It is possible to manage the job of edging grass with a spade and a plank of wood laid down as a guide for straight edges but the job is easier and neater with a sharp half moon. As the name suggests the tool is long handled with a metal head shaped like a rounded half moon.

Two completely different forms of hole maker, a **dibber** and a **mole** are also handy implements. The dibber, which can be as small as a shaped piece of dowelling or as large as the sharpened end of an old tool shaft, is used to make holes for individual seeds or seedlings such as cabbages.

The mole is a large metal screw on the end of a wooden handle which is driven into the ground to make holes sufficiently large to take fence posts or rustic poles. This tool makes an extremely neat job of excavating the right amount of soil for the job, where a spade would make a much larger than necessary hole.

If you intend to use sprays in the garden either to feed plants or kill pests and diseases, a **pump action sprayer** is useful. These come in a variety of forms and sizes, but if you take the organic or natural approach to gardening and eschew such products you will have little need of such a tool.

It is becoming increasingly popular to leave part of the garden in longer grass with a number of meadow plants and flowers to attract butterflies and insects. The grass however does need a twice yearly cut or harvest. A lawnmower would of course be completely wrong in this situation as even set on a long cut, it would shear the grass in an unacceptable way. You need instead a small single-handed scythe, known as a **sickle** or **grass hook**. Unlike the Old Father Time version this has a short curved blade which you use to cut the grass in a slicing motion. Cut away from your body or a momentary lapse in concentration could result in a nasty accident.

This completes my list of tool suggestions. There are many other more specialist tools on the market such as loppers, saws, trimmers and cultivators. It is unlikely when just beginning a garden that you will think these essential. If you do need a particular tool for just one job, try hiring rather than buying. Many motor maintenance centres are willing to hire out tools on a daily basis and if you can arrange to share with some neighbours the hire cost may work out relatively inexpensive.

Even the basic list of essential tools is a long and costly one so the next chapter looks at alternative methods of tool buying and suggests the best places to find a bargain.

4   WHERE TO BUY TOOLS

SHOPS

The most obvious places to look for new tools are department stores, garden centres and, increasingly, those large Do-It Yourself discount stores. Here you will shop in comfort, in warm and brightly-lit conditions. You will probably find a variety of broadly similar tools to choose from and, if you are lucky, the advice of sales assistants.

If you buy tools from such places they may be guaranteed for a certain period of time, giving you a come-back should anything go wrong, and if the tools are particularly large or unwieldy you may be able to have them delivered to your front door at little or no extra cost.

There may be promotional discounts on certain tools and sale bargains of old models or unseasonal items, but you will basically pay the full retail price of tools. You may be able to take advantage of credit facilities at a store so you can buy tools over a long period, but remember the interest charged can steeply increase costs. It is hardly worth going into hock for tools. Ideally your garden should be a peaceful retreat. If every time you cut the grass you are worried about paying off instalments on the lawnmower, you are unlikely to find it a source of relaxation.

Motor maintenance centres sometimes have reconditioned second-hand lawnmowers and other power tools available much more cheaply than you will find in the High Street stores. They also usually offer some form of guarantee – it is always worth enquiring if you are trying to cut costs.

AUCTIONS

As an alternative to shops you can be more adventurous and try your local auction centre. You will find advertisements for forthcoming sales in your local newspaper. Garden tools and furniture are normally sold along with general household goods but sometimes they are included in other sales, if for example they are being sold as part of a larger lot, perhaps after a stock clearance. If they are to be included in a sale, the notice in the newspaper will usually detail what is involved such as, 'two garden benches, one lawnmower, quantity of hand tools'. You are allowed to 'view', that is inspect, the items to be auctioned beforehand – this might be either the day before or on the morning of the sale. Do not expect a catalogue of entries, as these are only provided for more upmarket and expensive goods.

Auction rooms are not always the most salubrious of places. You will probably find the 'rooms' are housed in a large warehouse type of building, possibly a disused church. Dress warmly as it is often rather cold and airy because of the traffic of goods and people.

Viewing

You are free to look at and touch the goods unless there are notices to the contrary. Each item will be labeled with a number – this is the lot number. It will be called out by the auctioneer to identify the item at the time of sale. It may be that a porter will also hold the item aloft, but the sale proceeds according to lot number so it is best to note down any number you may be interested in. You won't be excused paying for something just because you have made a mistake in the lot numbers and ended up with a set of chairs instead of a lawnmower!

Viewing is extremely important. This is the time when you may spot a bargain and are given the opportunity to look it over. You should check to ensure that goods are working and up to the job. If you do not check by giving them a careful examination or by starting up a powered tool, if this is allowed, you are taking a chance. Obviously if the price is right and you are able to cope with do-it-yourself repairs it may be worth a gamble, otherwise your snip of a bargain may turn out a waste of money. Having said this, however, if you stick to non-power tools little should go wrong and bargains are often to be had at well below cost price.

Bidding

Make your mind up at the time of viewing how much you are prepared to spend on any item. Take into account its age, condition, and value to you. If you really have no idea of how much to bid and prices can be as low as fifty pence for a garden fork, attend a couple of auctions without bidding, just to get a feel for the prices. Having made your mind up as to how much you will bid, stick to it. Don't be tempted to 'up' your bid, thinking 'what's another pound?', as you could find yourself bidding much more than you originally intended.

You work out when any item you are interested in is likely to be sold by finding out how many lots the auctioneer deals with in an hour. There may be a sign saying when they expect to reach lot numbers 100, 200, 300 and so on. If not, ask – a porter will have a good idea of how long the sale normally takes. This saves standing around waiting for your lot number, while others are sold, which can be rather tedious. Plan to arrive at the auction about twenty minutes before your lot is due to be called, just to be on the safe side.

At the time of auction you will probably find yourself in a crowd of people, some of whom will be bargain hunters like yourself, others dealers, and yet others onlookers. If it is a general sale there is unlikely to be seating. You will have to stand amongst the goods to be sold waiting for your lot to be called.

The auctioneer may be on a small platform above the crowd and it as well to stand fairly close to him, where you can easily be seen. It would be silly to lose an item simply because your bid went unnoticed. Don't be afraid, either, that a simple scratch of the head or touch of your glasses will involve you in bidding for something you don't want. The auctioneer is as keen as anyone that the bids are genuine and if in doubt he will ask you if you meant to bid. It is usually sufficient simply to raise your hand.

The bidding may rise in units of one pound, two, five, or ten. Generally the auctioneer will try to start the bidding high, but the first accepted bid is the starting point from which you work. Don't be afraid to let the price drop right down before putting in your bid – you never know, perhaps no-one else will be interested and you will get a real bargain. Don't bother bidding if the competition is fierce. If more than two people are bidding the price will only rise more quickly, better to step in after someone falls out, if you are still interested. It may be that sometimes when you attend an auction you will not even place a bid, as the competition is too steep.

Auctions are exciting and you will no doubt feel your heart pounding as the auctioneer nears your lot number, but try to stay as calm as possible. Don't exceed your predetermined price limit. Don't be tempted either, into bidding for some object you have not previously inspected, just because the bidding seems ridiculously low. There may well be a reason for the price being low and you could end up with a 'pig in a poke'.

Sold! If you are successful in a bid the auctioneer will ask for your name and after a few minutes when the paper work has been processed you can pay for your item at the office simply by giving your name and lot number. You are then free to collect your goods and take them home. Obviously if what you have bought is rather large, you will have to wait until the end of the sale to collect it. Auctioneers often operate a transport service at an extra cost if you cannot get it home yourself.

Finally, it is important to keep your options open. It can be very disappointing to be too rigid about the order in which you plan to buy essential tools. If you really want a wheelbarrow, but there are none up for sale, be flexible and consider alternative tools you might need. Perhaps if the bidding is low you could buy a pair of lawn edgers instead and wait until the next auction in the hope of a wheelbarrow. Having said this however, don't buy just for the sake of it, because you have been infected with auction fever.

ADVERTISEMENTS

Another method of buying second-hand tools is to answer the classified advertisements in your local newspaper. Perfectly good tools can be bought this way. People are often keen to get rid of unwanted gifts in those columns which offer free advertising if the goods are below a certain price, often twenty-five pounds. You have the advantage of being able to take a good look at the item for sale and may even see a demonstration of it working. However, should you decide that for whatever reason, you don't want to buy, you can be at something of a disadvantage. You will probably have been invited into someone's home, have been offered a cup of tea and been made to feel welcome. After all this good will, it can seem rather churlish to refuse to buy and you may be embarrassed into buying something you are not really happy with. It pays to be aware of the danger and you should try to get as much information as possible over the telephone before going to see the goods. This may help avoid any potentially ticklish situations.

PRIVATE SALES

Finally, there are car boot and garage sales. These are increasingly popular methods of raising money both for individuals and charities. Car boot sales are normally held in a car park or field. For the cost of renting a space ordinary people as well as market traders can set up a stall, selling whatever they wish. The garage sale is, as the name suggests, normally the unwanted contents of someone's attic or garage, sold privately from their home.

It is worth scanning local news sheets for announcements of sales as all sorts of things can surface – often one man's poison turning out to be another man's new plant container! I recently bought, at a car boot sale, a handsome terracotta washbowl to plant bulbs in and a large black enamelled tub for use as a shrub pot, for the princely sum of seventy-five pence.

Don't be afraid to bargain with the sellers as they are usually anxious to get rid of their things, the sale often being part of their spring cleaning. They are normally good natured affairs which include a lot of banter and exclamations over long forgotten 'treasure'. You can't be lucky every time but if you enjoy the hunt for a bargain, I'm sure you will enjoy these open air jumbles.

5 PREPARING, PLANTING AND PROPAGATING

PREPARING THE GARDEN

This is it then – by now you should have a detailed plan of your ideal garden. You will know where you plan to site the key features such as patio, paths, border contours and areas of planting. You will also have sites in mind for the rubbish bin, compost heap, clothes drier and any other necessities of your life such as the wood pile, coal bunker or rabbit hutch, and you have assembled a stock of essential tools.

Now that you can actually make a start the first priority is either to erect or check fencing. Nothing can be more disheartening than to see a carefully worked border full of plants flattened by a fence blown over in strong winds. Not only does the fence do damage in falling but by the time you have repaired or replaced it your border will be well trampled. If necessary, protect your fences with preservative – one which will not harm plants.

Do all those jobs which mean treading on the soil, for example digging holes for fence posts, before you attempt to work the soil itself. Doing it in any other order simply means twice as much work as the soil becomes compacted under your weight.

This is the prime time to site your garden essentials like the shed and clothes drier and construct your patio and paths. If you want to alter the shape of existing paths or remove them altogether this is also the time to do it. If you have to remove a path, the rubble might come in handy for foundations of a patio or new paths.

Foundations   If your paths are to take anything but the lightest of traffic you should be prepared to give them a foundation. It is important that paths are firm and stable. They must be able to support both your weight and that of a loaded wheelbarrow without subsiding or buckling. It is infuriating always to be caught by a raised paving stone when struggling with a heavy barrow. About four to six inches of hard packed rubble, topped with a few inches of sand should be enough to give you a firm basis on which to lay slabs. If you plan to drive over the path you will obviously need a deeper foundation. For ease of mowing make sure the level of paths is just below the level of the lawn.

If your path or patio is to run alongside the house be sure not to bridge the damp course or you will create problems inside.

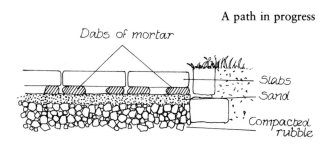

A path in progress

When laying your slabs, use a spirit level to ensure your work is level, and keep slabs firmly in place by using a dab of mortar in each corner and in the middle. Try to take your time. Work at your own pace so that you do not overtire yourself with, perhaps, unaccustomed labour: little will be gained if you complete the job ahead of schedule but spend the following week in bed resting a bad back.

Try to complete as much of the construction work as you can afford before starting on the garden proper. This will not only give you a feeling of accomplishment and maybe somewhere to sit even if the rest of the garden is barren, but it will minimise any possible damage to plants you plan to establish.

Don't despair, however, if you simply can't afford to do all you plan in one fell swoop. Complete the paths so they can take traffic across the garden and perhaps leave the patio or seating area as grass meantime. It seems better to economise in this way, deferring projects, rather than doing everything in cheaper material than first envisaged. Inevitably such savings are something of a disappointment and you end up spending more money redoing the job later.

Borders

When it comes to laying down the shapes of borders for the first time or reshaping existing beds, you have a choice. Your plan may dictate large beds spreading over many square yards, but you know you cannot stand the cost of all the plants you wish to buy. One option is to go ahead and make the beds as you ideally wish them, facing the fact you will have a lot of bare earth to look at and a lot of weeding to do to keep the area clean. The advantages are that you will not be constantly eating away at the edge of a smaller border to increase its size and thus having to move plants forward, and that you will also be able to weed and dig the bed over as a whole.

Alternatively, while still following the overall design of your planned border, you could create a smaller border which you can afford to stock with plants. Against this of course is the fact that you will have to be prepared to change the border, move, and perhaps discard, plants as the garden progresses.

Personally I favour the compromise of establishing relatively large borders according to plan, digging, weeding and feeding the soil when it is empty of plants, and then selecting a few key plants to buy. You may already have a tree in mind for the border, so that is an obvious place to start. Buy as many of the other permanent plants as you can afford, and begin to introduce cheaper ground cover to grow over the earth meantime. This will help the area have a more established look and smother weed growth at the same time. The ground-hugging plants like the periwinkles and ivies are all easily propogated so you only need buy one of each type and multiply the plants yourself.

If you cannot afford even this budget planting scheme you might prefer to leave areas of the garden wild rather than create foot wide borders all the way round the garden. Tiny borders never look impressive, support little growth and are so fiddly as to be hardly worth the effort. Better be positive and accept your present limitations working only one area of the garden at a time than spread your resources just too thinly. If anyone raises an eyebrow at your 'wild' areas leave them in no doubt that they are meant to be like that, as you are doing your bit for ecology.

Shaping Borders

When creating the borders try to avoid the straight lines which make grass cutting more of a chore. Create contours to lead the eye in and out of areas so that, when established, the garden will have hidden pockets. A garden hose is a useful aid when experimenting with possible shapes. Lay it on the ground and continue changing it until you are satisfied with the line. If you are confident, you can then mark the line with a spade, taking care not to puncture the hose. If, however, it is likely to be some time before grass is put down to meet the border's edge, mark the line with pegs and string. Pegs need be no more than fillets of wood about one foot in length. Drive them into the ground following the line you have chosen and wind the string round them.

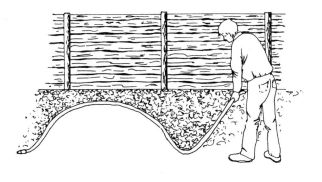

Getting the right shape

Digging at last! You can now get started on the hard work and dig over the areas designated as borders. If you have chosen to construct a vegetable garden the advice is just the same. No matter what you intend to grow, you must put in some effort to get the hoped-for results.

Brambles and perennial weeds like nettles, docks and buttercups must be completely dug out. Try to get out every last piece of root or they will only reappear to strangle some poor plant. It is best to bag up such weeds for disposal as they really are too sneaky to put on the compost heap.

When To Dig The ideal time for digging is in late autumn when nature will help with some of the work. If you can manage just to turn the soil over roughly, any hard frosts you might have will help break up the clods of earth further. However, whichever season you find yourself in, don't waste your time by trying to dig wet sodden soil. You won't help your cause and might endanger your heart in the process.

Wait until the soil is dry and work backwards from your starting point to avoid walking over and recompacting worked soil. There is very little which is instant in gardening and digging does take time. It can, however, be a very satisfying activity. If you don't believe me, wait until you can step back to smugly view an area of freshly turned, weed-free soil which is a result of your endeavours.

Soil Types If you do not already know, it will become apparent while digging exactly which soil type you have. Soils vary enormously. If you have loam in your garden, that is that dark, rich soil which crumbles cleanly through your fingers, you will wonder what all the fuss is about. You will be able to dig it easily, work it at almost any time of the year and of course grow bumper crops and glorious flowers. If you are less fortunate you might find you have clay, easily recognisable as it bakes as hard as concrete in the summer, while being sticky and sodden in the winter. At the other end of the spectrum are sandy soils which dry out quickly and are unable to maintain any richness.

No soil, thankfully, is without merit. Clay is rich and capable of sustaining great plant growth, while sandy soils have the advantage of being easily worked and warming up quickly in the spring. If you have soil that is special because it is very peaty and acidic, or on the other hand very chalky and limey, pay special attention to your choice of plants. Study what is growing locally, and talk to your neighbours with already established gardens. If you stick with plants which enjoy your special conditions they will flourish, it is only when you try to introduce 'foreigners' that things can get a bit difficult. As always if you aim to work with rather than against nature life is a lot easier.

Improving Your Soil

Whatever kind of soil you have, work will improve it. Clay needs to be opened up to make it easier to work, to improve its drainage and to prevent the soil particles sticking together, so improving its structure. Dig in almost anything you have to hand such as ash from the fire, coffee grinds, tea leaves, pea gravel, broken shells, washed sand and crushed rubble. For a lasting improvement dig in as much compost and well rotted manure as possible.

Organic matter, animal and plant, really is the key to improving all soil types. It helps bulk out clay and by rotting down improves the fertility and water-retaining properties of sand, and makes sure loam retains its health. Magical muck: if you live in the country, arrange with a local farmer or riding stable to deliver a ton of manure at least once and preferably twice a year in the spring and autumn. If well rotted manure is unavailable make do with fresh, allowing it to rot away on the compost heap.

When you are in the initial stages of preparing a garden and are unhindered by plants and root systems you can dig organic matter in all over, in vast quantities, thereafter use it only on cleared ground and as a mulch round plants where it will both feed the plant and suppress weed growth.

If you can't obtain any manure consider the alternatives. Both mushroom compost and peat can be used and both are light and easy to handle, although more expensive than farm-yard manure. If you have nothing else use your own garden compost and leaf mould – there is nothing wrong with this but it is difficult to produce in sufficient quantities for a whole garden and you have to wait for it to come on 'tap'.

After you have dug over and worked in the organic matter leave the soil to settle for a few weeks before planting if possible. While the digging is going on you will become increasingly aware of the idiosyncracies of your garden. You will find out where the dampest and coldest areas are, your sunniest spots, those parts which are sheltered and those where the wind whistles through. Take note of these points and use them to revise your planting plan if necessary, so that you put plants in the positions they will appreciate most. You might realise for example that a sun-loving rose has been planned for a border which spends most of the day in shade, or you intend to put a hosta which likes to be cool and shady in a sunny spot.

BUYING TREES AND SHRUBS

After making any necessary adjustments to your plan you can decide on which plants to buy first. If you have a particular problem to solve, such as lack of privacy, or noise, you will want to tackle this as a priority, either by erecting a screen over which you may plan to have climbers or by planting a hedge. Generally, however, the first plants to go in are those which will make the biggest visual impact in the garden, namely trees and large shrubs.

Depending upon the time of year, you may have the choice between buying bare-root or container-grown plants. Bare-root plants, some of which are so fresh that they are only lifted from the ground by the nurseryman when you buy, are generally cheaper but are only suitable for planting during the dormant season between November and March. Container-grown plants, although more expensive are available all year round and can be planted at your leisure. If you are tempted to buy a container-grown plant on impulse, however, and do not have time to plant it for a week or so, don't leave it standing in an exposed position. It is all too easily toppled over and branches can be damaged or broken.

Whether you choose to buy container-grown trees or are able to use bare-root, trees are expensive long term investments which deserve a little consideration. There are no magical rituals to observe when planting but if you use common sense and put some effort into preparing the ground the trees will appreciate and repay you for the labour.

PLANTING BARE-ROOT PLANTS

Unless you plan to plant bare-root trees or shrubs as soon as you get them home, you will have to give them some form of temporary quarters. If for instance you plan to plant your new plant the next day all you need do is put it into a bucket of water to give the roots a good soak. Don't risk freezing the

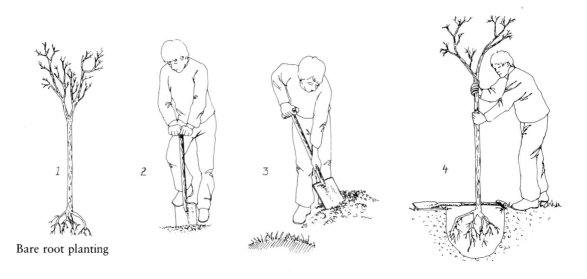

Bare root planting

plant and keep it out of chill winds and draughts by storing it in a garage or shed overnight. All plants which arrive bare-root, especially those delivered through the post, will in any case appreciate a reviving drink before planting and you should plan to soak them for at least a few hours before planting.

If on the other hand you have to delay planting for more than a day, you should dig out a trench deep enough to accommodate the new plant and cover the roots with soil. If this is impossible, perhaps because the ground is frozen hard, keep the plant inside, protected from the frost and cover the roots in moist peat or compost covered with sacking.

In a new garden you may already have dug over and worked organic matter into the whole of your border, and this is ideal. But even if you are working within an established border don't try to skimp on effort and materials by simply digging a hole big enough to accommodate a new tree and no more. You should try to dig over an area two or three times as large as the root spread on the tree. Your hole should be large enough to easily take the spread of roots, and at least one and a half times the depth of the roots.

Put to one side the earth which has been excavated and break up the soil at the bottom of the hole, adding compost or organic matter as you work. Add and mix organic matter with the soil taken from the hole as well and after putting back a spadeful or so, try resting the tree back in the hole to see if you have the correct depth. As a check place a hoe or other long-handled tool across the top of the hole. The old earth level on the tree will be shown by a ring around the trunk. When the hoe and the ring on the tree are level you have the correct depth at which to plant the tree. It might take a bit of perseverance and it is definitely easier if there are two people working together, but it is worth getting right.

When the level has been established, take the tree out of the hole again and drive in a support stake, slightly off centre and behind where the trunk of the tree will be. The stake should be about the same height as the trunk of the tree before it breaks into branches.

The tree can now be put back into the hole for the last time. If possible get someone to hold it for you and stand back to view it. Make sure you will see it from its best side and when satisfied carefully arrange the roots in the hole and around the stake. Snip off and remove any roots which have been damaged. While the tree is still being held, refill the hole with the enriched soil firming it into place with heel of your boot. Attach the tree to the stake, rake level the soil, water the tree in and add a mulch to the earth at the foot of the tree. Now all you need do is rake smooth any footprints left in the soil and stand back to admire your handiwork.

PLANTING

CONTAINER-BOUGHT PLANTS

The preparation of the soil is exactly the same for trees bought in containers as for bare-root trees but it is sometimes easier to stake a container-tree at a distance of several inches to avoid damaging the rootball, after the specimen has been planted.

Container-grown trees should be well watered while still in their containers, as this makes them easier to remove from the pot. You should be able to slit the sides of the container with a sharp knife. Watch your fingers as the edges can be very sharp. Prise the container away from the tree after putting it into its new home but don't attempt to free or tease out the roots. After completely removing the container, return the soil to the hole, firm in place with the heel of your boot and carefully stake the tree. Give the tree a further watering and level and mulch the surrounding ground.

Follow the same procedure for planting shrubs, although you will probably not need to stake them. The same rules apply when moving large plants about the garden. If you lift them with a fairly large clump of soil about their roots, simply treat them as container-grown plants and they should move quite happily.

To Summarise There are no secrets to planting trees or shrubs and you need not be daunted by the prospect. Simply prepare a decently sized area of ground, add organic matter, stake if necessary and remember to water. Watering is especially important for plants put in in the spring. While they establish themselves in the hottest months of the year, you should be prepared to give them ample supplies of water. This does not mean the odd pintful now and again, but allowing the hose to water the area surrounding new planting for at least an hour, as often as necessary to prevent the soil from drying out.

Never forget to remove the plant container

CREATING THE LAWN

You may now want to think about creating a new lawn. Lawns can either be sown or turfed immediately after the trees and major shrubs have been planted, or you can wait until the rest of the planting has been done. The choice really depends on how much time you have, how much you can afford to spend on planting and the time of year.

Sowing grass seed is obviously much cheaper than buying an 'instant' lawn from turfs, but you must sow at the correct time of year. This is either late summer/early autumn – August/September or in late spring – April/May.

Preparation

Clear the ground of weed and rubble

Sowing or turfing grass means quite a bit of preparation beforehand. In either case you must clear the ground of all rubble and weed, dig it thoroughly and feed with organic matter, preferably manure. If you can, it is then best to allow the ground to settle naturally for 3–4 weeks. Following this, you start a programme of fining down and levelling the soil. First, using a fork or spade, break down the clods of earth and remove any stones which have worked their way to the surface, then rake over the earth. Now comes the 'fun' part, or at least it is fun for any neighbours who may witness your antics. You have to firm the soil down by treading over it. It's best to do this by putting your weight on your heels and by taking tiny steps work your way back and forth until all the earth has been flattened.

A lawn or general purpose fertiliser should now be applied. Follow the directions on the packet, and don't be tempted to increase the dosage in the hope that it will spur grass on ahead of time – it won't do any good.

Finally, you have to rake the area yet again to achieve a fine level surface. Make sure that the soil is dry enough to work or you will end up paddling in a mud bath instead of achieving the fine surface important for the finished lawn. Take your time over this final rake. Don't try to hurry the process on by leaning far over with the rake and taking great bites out of the earth. This is a sure way to end up with a bad temper and a sore back. Use the rake lightly, work on a small patch and gently smooth out the very top of the earth.

That's it then, now you are ready to grass. The process of preparation is admittedly fairly long but it is not a complicated procedure. However, if you have a very big area to grass you might want to tackle it in parts or enlist help, either from willing friends or by hiring mechanical help.

If your aim is to create a wildflower lawn from seed, the process is somewhat simpler. You do not have to enrich or fertilise the soil but you have nevertheless to dig over the area to remove weeds and, if necessary, improve drainage.

Sowing Grass Seed

There are grass seed mixes to suit all needs. For a lawn to be used by a family you will want a utility mix which includes some really tough grasses. For a fine lawn there are luxury mixes and yet other mixtures for problem areas such as shade under trees. There are also a number of wildflower and meadow seed mixtures which include special varieties for clay, chalk and loam soils. When sowing such mixtures it is as well to bulk the seed out with something like sand. The seed varies a great deal and this helps to ensure even distribution.

Take all the help nature offers and choose a calm, dry day to sow to avoid seed being lost in the wind. Rake over the top gently to accommodate the seed and mark out what a square

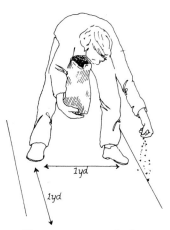

You can use your body as a rough guide for seed sowing

yard looks like. You can easily do this with garden canes. If you feel nervous you can sub-divide the whole area to be seeded into strips a yard wide and then mark it across into square yards by drawing a line in the soil with a cane.

Next weigh out the amount of seed you will need for a square yard. Don't add any for luck but stick to the recommended amount. You can then weigh out what you will need to sow a strip of ground. Alternatively, if you can recognise the amount of seed needed for each square yard in terms of a handful, you can dispense with the scales.

If you cannot be bothered to mark out your future lawn in squares, you can roughly judge a square yard using your body as a guide. Stand in a relaxed position with your feet apart and lean over at the hips with your arms outstretched. If you sow into the area between the reach of your arms and your feet you will not be far out. Try to sow the seed as evenly as possible. If you have any qualms practise on a piece of newspaper first, then you won't waste any seed.

To finish the job off, lightly rake the area over to cover up the seed. The seed is attractive to birds and you might want to rig up some form of deterrent – but whatever you do and however many dangling milk bottle tops you suspend, it seems you have to accept some loss. Now all you have to do is wait for the grass to grow – not forgetting to water well when necessary. Don't allow the soil to dry out from the time you sow until the grass is well established.

When the grass is about two inches long you can get the mower out. Just shave the top off, using the blades on the highest setting and gradually over the season, lower the cutting height. If your lawn is going to be hard used don't ever cut it too short but keep it between three quarters and one inch long.

Inevitably weeds will show up in the lawn but most will disappear when you start mowing. Unless you are a lawn fetishist, I would be content to leave things like that. However if you enjoy poring over grass on your hands and knees you could try hand weeding, being careful not to dislodge the new grass, to get rid of every last weed. Alternatively you could use a chemical but you will have to look for one specially intended for treating young lawns.

Turf Just as there are different kinds of grass seed so there are differences in quality and price of turf. It pays to shop around for what you want. If you see turf advertised particularly cheaply be suspicious as it may be little more than field grass which has been cut a few times.

Arrange to have the turf delivered no more than two days before you plan to lay it. If you have to store it for more than 48 hours you should take it out of its rolls and stack it grass side up, keeping it moist until you can use it.

Turfs being laid like bricks

When you do lay the turf handle it gently. You do not want to tear or damage it unnecessarily. If you can, work from a straight edge, laying the turfs one next to another. Stagger the second row of turfs, if necessary starting with a half turf, so the lawn takes on the appearance of a brick wall. Butt the pieces together and firm into place with the back of a rake to make sure the turf is in contact with the soil. Overlap the contours of your border so you can cut round with a heavy sharp knife or half-moon edger when you have laid the whole lawn.

If it becomes apparent that there are small bumps and indents under some of the turfs, simply lift them and either excavate or add more soil as necessary.

Finally, you might like to make doubly sure all is well by using two planks of wood to walk over the lawn. Simply walk along the length of the planks, first one then the other, moving them until you have covered the entire lawn. This makes certain that the turfs are in position and well laid.

As with seed, wait until the turfs have established themselves before mowing and gradually lower the cutting blades of the mower over the season. You should also keep a careful watch during dry spells to ensure the ground is never allowed to dry out.

GROWING YOUR OWN PLANTS
FROM SEED

Your garden will certainly be taking shape when the lawn is down, and even if you already have a framework of trees and shrubs you will no doubt wish to further increase your plant collection. The cheapest way of doing this is, undoubtedly, by growing your own plants from seed.

Don't be put off by your first glance through a seed catalogue. As well as the attractive descriptions there can be a myriad of strange and confusing terms – annuals, half-hardies, hardies, perennials, biennials, hybrids, F1's. Don't panic, it is really quite simple. The most basic distinction is between those seeds which are sown outside in open ground and those which need some warmth to germinate. Most hardy annuals can be sown outside while half hardy annuals are generally started with a little heat.

To sow seeds outside you need to get your soil in good order first. Although every gardener is an optimist you cannot expect miracles: it is no good pressing seeds into hard caked clods of earth and expecting them to flourish. You should aim for a soil which is a good dark brown colour and which can be crumbled between your fingers. Work as much organic matter into the earth as you can. Dig it over thoroughly, removing weed and debris and then rake it level, allowing it to settle for a few days if you can afford the time.

Sowing

Vegetables are usually sown in rows along shallow drills. Flower seed is normally scattered in bold clumps. If you plan to sow a number of different flower seeds in a border it is helpful to mark off the area for each particular seed type by drawing lines with a cane in the soil or by marking with trails of sand.

Sow evenly and thinly, covering the seed with soil to the depth recommended on the seed packet. Don't tread the soil down or you risk caking the surface, making it resistant to moisture.

Thinning

After a period of anything up to about four weeks the seedlings will begin to appear. When they have grown to a size which you can easily handle, make your first thinning to remove excess plants. At the first thinning you might plan on leaving between two and three inches between seedlings.

After a few weeks you can thin the plants for a second time to achieve the spacing recommended on the packet. Removing plants in this way might seem very wasteful but it is necessary to allow the remaining plants sufficient room to mature. If you overcrowd plants they tend to develop into rather poor leggy specimens. You can cut down on the waste, however, by sowing as thinly as possible in the first place. Some of the vegetables thinned can also be eaten, such as immature lettuce, turnips or beetroot.

Biennials

If you plan to grow large numbers of biennials, that is, seeds sown one year for flowering the next, such as pansies and honesty, you might like to use a special nursery bed. This means that you will not lose border space to young plants which have little show value. You can use that space for other more attractive plants while growing the biennials in ground perhaps hived off from the vegetable patch.

Sow the seeds in rows, thin out and grow on until they are ready to be moved to their final flowering position. The young plants should generally be in position by mid to late autumn to allow them to establish themselves before the weather becomes too severe. You will probably be lifting tired summer bedding by the beginning of September in any case.

Outdoor Cover for Seeds

Just because seeds can grow outside without any special help does not mean you cannot offer them a helping hand to ensure success. This might be something as simple as laying down strips of plastic sheeting held in place with stones, to cover the earth where seeds will be sown. By doing this at the beginning of the year you make sure the soil is drier and warmer than it would be naturally. This allows you to work it more quickly and enables you to get a better tilth. If you follow this with a simple cloche, which need be no more than hoops of wire supporting a tunnel of polythene sheeting, you can get seeds and young plants off to a flying start.

The protection a cloche affords from wet and cold enables you to sow seeds earlier than you otherwise could. The young plants are then brought on in the sheltered environment to mature earlier than normal. This is important with vegetables as it extends the cropping season. Flowers benefit too as they can be brought into early bloom.

Seed Trays

Some seeds need even more protection than a cloche can offer. Those seeds which need to be germinated in warmth should be sown into a seed tray. On a small scale you can use any shallow containers you might have, or buy cheap lightweight trays sold for the purpose. There are also heavier-weight plastic trays available which last several years although they obviously cost more. If you are simply dipping your toe into the business of seed sowing, you might just as well use clean household containers, such as old margarine tubs. Make sure you make drainage holes in the bottom of them before you start.

Don't use ordinary garden soil, or you could end up with a pot full of weed. Buy a ready-mixed compost. There is no need, really, to use a special type just for seed, a multi-purpose compost will do. Buy a bag just large enough to suit your purpose. It is a false economy to buy an over-large size as the fresher compost is, the better, and you don't want to keep it from year to year.

Now comes the messy part, and, if you are not working in a shed or outside, you might like to spread a liberal layer of newspaper around the area of the kitchen sink. Fill your clean container with compost, lightly tapping and firming it in place. Use the base of a similarly sized container to gently press it down. This gets rid of air pockets and gives you a good level surface for sowing.

Sow the seeds thinly as directed on the packet. If the seeds are really tiny you might like to bulk them out with a little sand which makes them easier to sow and shows you where you have already sown. Cover them over with compost as directed

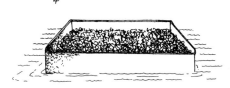

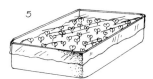

Sowing seed in trays

on the seed packet and immerse the whole tray up to its shoulders in water. Count to ten and water should appear on the surface of the compost. This works both to pull the seeds down into firm contact with the compost and gives them a good wetting at the same time. Now set the tray aside to drain.

When it is sufficiently dry, label the container so that you know which seeds are which, cover with a taut film of transparent self-adhesive film of the sort used to keep food fresh and pop it into the airing cupboard.

The whole process is very simple, quick and easy. You should be careful to ensure, however, that everything you use is scrupulously clean. Fungus can attack young seedlings, causing them to keel over and die and it seems that the best way of avoiding trouble is by keeping trays, pots and dibbers as clean as possible. You can also help prevent the trouble by using a fresh compost, sowing thinly and not over-watering the seeds. However if the worst comes to the worst, you can use a chemical diluted in water. It might not save affected seeds but should prevent damage happening to other trays.

Back in the airing cupboard, the seeds will be beginning to germinate. Keep an eye on them, and as soon as you can see some growth, bring them out into the light. First appearances will be tiny white shoots with a yellow tip, something like a bean shoot. The tray will probably still hold moisture but check to make sure and add more water if necessary. Now put the tray on a light windowsill. Protect the seedlings from extremes: don't let them be crisped by the sun or frozen by draughts at night. You will also have to turn the tray around so that the plants do not become bent towards the light. After the second, or true leaves appear, from which you can identify the plant, you can begin to sort or prick them out.

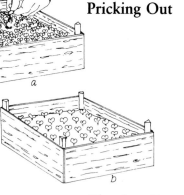

Pricking Out Use a disinfected plastic plant label or the tip of a pencil to raise the seedling, roots and all, from the compost. Be gentle and try not to cause too much disturbance within the tray. To do this, handle the seedling by its leaves, not the stem, in case you break it. Remove it completely from the tray. Make a small hole large enough to accommodate its roots in the pot or tray of compost to which it is being moved. Gently place the seedling in its new home, and press the compost back in place using your fingers. When you have filled the container, giving each seedling room for growth, water and grow on, watering whenever the surface of the compost appears dry.

Planting Out Don't be in too much of a hurry to plant out your seedlings. It is quite a change from life on the windowsill to life outside, and you should try to make the transition as easily and gradually as possible.

Assuming you don't have access to a greenhouse or any means of outside protection you can begin by simply placing your seed trays outside on warm days. Be careful to keep watering up, as the seedlings can quickly dry out in the shallow trays. Bring the trays back inside towards evening when the temperature starts to fall. Gradually increase the period spent outside, until you are happy to leave them outside all night. Watch the weather forecasts and don't begin until the danger of frost is over.

To be on the safe side, you can cover the pots and trays with a layer of newspaper. Keep them off the ground by putting them onto a piece of wood supported by bricks or on top of a handy coal bunker.

Making a Cold Frame Seeds derive more protection from a cold frame, which makes the business of hardening them off simpler. A frame is a basic sort of mini greenhouse. There are many models available on the market, with either glass or hard plastic glazing topping a wooden or brick-sided box. It is possible, however, to make your own version very cheaply indeed.

You will need to get hold of a couple of old orange boxes and a length of polythene. Your local greengrocer may be happy to part with such boxes free of charge if you are a good customer, although some have started charging small sums for them.

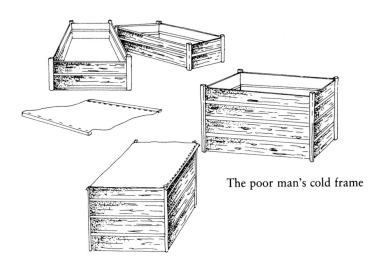

The poor man's cold frame

To make one frame you will need two boxes. Remove the bottom from one and fit it over the other, securing it in place with nails if necessary. Cover with a strong piece of polythene, to which you have previously stapled a piece of wood along the bottom edge. This cover can be held in place with a loop of garden wire.

Your frame won't be the most elegant garden adornment, nor will it work as well as shop-bought models, but it is cheap and it will afford your plants some protection. To increase its efficiency you can line the bottom of the frame with a wodge of old newspapers, but these deteriorate quickly. If you can, use the polystyrene chips sometimes used to pack goods in, or the bubble film which sometimes comes around china.

If you do use a cold frame, make sure it is sited in an open site but not in full sun. The plants can be hardened by gradually opening up the top cover and eventually leaving it off all night.

By the time plants are fully hardened off they will be filling their seed trays and raring to go. The ground should have been prepared in advance with a good amount of organic matter already dug in and raked smooth.

Get down on your knees or squat by the border so that you are close to your work. Using a trowel excavate a small hole ready to house a seedling. Have your tray of seedlings to hand. It helps if they have just been watered in the tray as it makes them looser and easier to remove. Handling a seedling by its leaves, pop it into the hole and firm it into place with your fingers, patting the soil with the back of your trowel.

Start at the back of the border and work forwards, spacing the plants as recommended, so that you avoid treading on newly planted seedlings. When you have finished play the hose gently over the whole area to give them a good wetting. If it happens to be very sunny, however, wait until the sun goes down before watering or you will risk burning the seedlings.

Providing you water them when necessary, they should now grow away quite happily, providing you with vegetables and flowers that are all your own work.

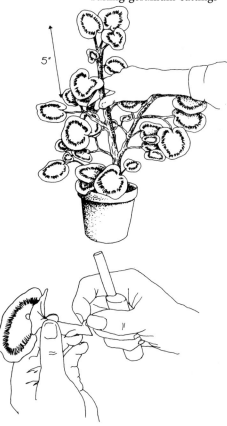

Taking geranium cuttings

CUTTINGS

Along with seeds, cuttings must be one of the cheapest methods of getting new plants. There are a number of methods of taking cuttings: at different times of the year, and also of different sections of the plant, such as softwood, semi-ripe, hardwood cuttings and pipings.

Semi-Ripe Start with something easy, such as a geranium (*Pelargonium*) – you might have one on a windowsill you can experiment with. Geraniums root quickly and easily from semi-ripe cuttings, so providing a useful source of next year's summer bedding.

Ideally the cuttings should be taken between July and August. Using a sharp clean knife cut a shoot which is hard at the base but still soft at the top. It should be about 5 inches long. Make the cut just below a leaf joint and remove the lower leaves, which would simply rot beneath the compost. Some people now advocate leaving these cuttings to dry out for about an hour before planting up.

Put about three cuttings into a pot using a branded compost, then water and put onto a bright windowsill. Take care not to overwater, and leave well alone. You will know all is well if the tops remain healthy. When you see signs of growth they will have rooted properly. If necessary you can then pot the cuttings up into individual pots.

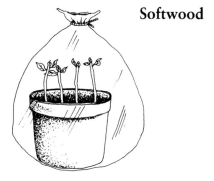

Soft and hard wood cuttings

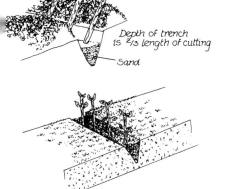

Depth of trench is ⅔ length of cutting

Sand

Softwood

Many shrubs can be propagated from softwood cuttings. These are taken early in the year, up to early summer, from the soft growing tips of plants. With a friend's consent it is worth snipping the tips off any fancied plants to see if you have any success. Cut the tips with a sharp knife and pop them straight into a plastic bag to prevent them drying out.

When you get home trim the cuttings to about three inches long just below a leaf joint. Remove the lower leaves and just touch the base of the stem into a hormone rooting powder, tapping off excess powder on the edge of the tub. You can then insert the cuttings into compost. Put a number around the edge of a pot, allowing just enough space so that they are not touching one another. Firm each in place with your fingers and water them in.

After allowing the pot to drain, place the whole thing inside a plastic bag. Inflate the bag so that it is not resting on the cuttings and tie the top with a twist of wire. Bags sold for home freezing are ideal as they come with their own twists of wire and sticky labels for naming. It is important to keep up the humidity of softwood cuttings, but watch out for rot. Allow the bag to open up several times a week to allow fresh air in.

Leave the pot on a warm windowsill, perhaps above a radiator. Don't be too anxious to tip the pot out to see if the cuttings are rooting. If you are patient you will see signs of growth which show rooting has taken place. You can then grow the cuttings on, potting them up individually and hardening the new plants off when they are of a size to be planted out.

Hardwood

Hardwood cuttings taken at the end of the year are probably the simplest cuttings of all. In fact you could try rooting up the prunings of roses and some will usually take. Whether it is a rose or other shrub, look for hard stemmy wood. You will find suitable pieces for cuttings on small branches which have grown out of established stems in the previous season.

Take cuttings between eight and twelve inches in length and remove bottom buds and leaves. Dig a trench deep enough to accommodate about two thirds of the length of the cuttings. You might like to put down a layer of sand in the bottom to encourage rooting and then insert the cuttings. Put the earth back, firm down and leave well alone. If you are lucky, given a few seasons these stems will form new plants for you.

Pipings Pipings are a special type of cutting used to propagate pinks. In late summer simply pull out the centre leaves from the young shoots of established plants. You will find a little V-shape of leaves comes away in your hand. Carefully remove the bottom leaves and insert the remaining leaves or pipings into a pot of well draining compost. Place the pot in a shaded cold frame if you have one or simply leave to root up in a sheltered part of the garden, being careful not to let them dry out.

DIVISION

Another method of increasing plants is root division. Nothing could be simpler or quicker than this method of propagation as you don't even have to wait to see new clumps of plants emerge before your eyes.

Perhaps the simplest method of root division is the one suitable for polyanthus. Lift a large plant, which you want to split up, with as much root as you can. It does not matter if you lift a large amount of soil at the same time as this is all going to be washed off. Put the plant into a bucket of water and leave it for a good soak. This will remove most of the earth from the roots, making them clearly visible and easy to prise apart. You will see from the top of the plant where the new plants have been formed. Split the mother plant into its various pieces using your fingers. Each part, apart from the oldest middle section, can now be planted up separately. This division is best done immediately after the plant has flowered to give the new young individual plants time to establish themselves for the following spring.

You can divide many of the herbaceous border plants in late autumn by root division. Larger plants, where it is impractical to try to immerse them in water, are best divided after lifting with a sharp knife or spade. It is often advocated that you should use two garden forks, back to back, to prise clumps apart. But even if you have two forks it must be one of the most difficult ways of doing it! As long as you ensure that each piece of plant to be planted up has a good portion of root attached you should experience no trouble, and soon you will be wondering what to do with all your plants.

6   100 TIPS FOR ECONOMISING

This list of one hundred tips aims to stretch your budget and your gardening imagination even further.

- When watering grow-bags, add a drop of washing-up liquid to the water. This will help retain moisture in the grow-bag.

- Use old tin foil containers, such as those supplied by takeaway restaurants, for propagating seeds. Simply make sure that they are thoroughly clean, spike the base for drainage, and fill with suitable compost. Large seeds like beans and sweet peas can even be sown individually into small cream or yoghurt cartons. The clear plastic type of cup dispensed by drinks machines can be used to top such containers, so in effect you create a mini propagator to encourage the seed to burst into life. If you do decide to use old plastic containers, try piercing the base with a hot skewer, which will penetrate the plastic more easily and safely than a sharp knife.

- Toilet roll tubes can be used to grow seeds such as sweet peas, which develop long roots. Plant the seeds into compost-filled tubes and grow on as normal. Give the tube a good wetting before planting outside so that roots can penetrate the soil easily.

- When sowing tiny seeds don't waste money by over sowing; you will only have to discard large numbers of seedlings when the seeds could probably be saved for sowing another year. Sow thinly, using a pepper pot to tap the seed out onto the compost, or mix the seed with white sand before sowing. This has the added advantage of showing where the seed has fallen.

- Save unused seeds for another year by storing them in cool, dry, dark conditions. You may not have a one hundred per cent success rate, but you will have sufficient success for the average gardener, particularly if you sow into a tray rather than outside. Alternatively, swap unused seeds with friends. Your friends will undoubtedly reciprocate and that way you will build up a variety of seed at no additional cost.

- Join your local gardening society. You will probably be able to spot a poster at your library or perhaps an advertisement in your weekly paper will announce their next talk or meeting. For usually a small joining fee you will not only meet like-minded people interested in gardening, benefit from shared knowledge and experienced speakers, but also be in a position to take up any money-saving offers on cheaper seeds, compost or fertiliser.

- Don't be over anxious to weed. Self-sown seedlings either dropped by passing birds or distributed by neighbouring plants can often be grown *in situ* or lifted and nurtured more carefully in a pot, once again increasing stock without cost.

- If you have an old disused child's play house discard the outer plastic skin and make use of the remaining house or cage to construct a mini greenhouse or frame. By covering mine in clear polythene, which I secured to the frame by means of washing line pegs, I was able to harden off plants satisfactorily for bedding and then cover and mature tomato plants in a sheltered spot.

- Help speed up the germination of seeds with a particularly hard outer coating, such as sweet peas. Either nick the coating with a sharp knife (watching your fingers) or abrade with a piece of sandpaper. Do not remove all the coating, just enough to glimpse the seed beneath.

- Send for all free seed catalogues. They are usually packed with ideas and useful hints, and at the very least make enjoyable winter reading when you can get on with nothing else in the garden.

- Order seeds early. You can sometimes take advantage of money-saving offers if you order by a certain date. Look out, too, for any special offers on bulk purchases. It may be possible to get together with friends or neighbours to put a bulk order in. This can result in a multiple saving on initial cost, postage and unnecessary duplication of seed orders.

- Take advantage of advertisements promoting products through competitions. You often need not make any purchase to enter such competitions and you never know, you might just win!

- When planting peas, include small sprigs of gorse in the seed drill to try to cut down on losses. In theory the gorse should help deter mice who will otherwise steal the pea seeds.

- Encourage the children to earn their pocket money by getting them to string milk bottle tops or strips of plastic cut from supermarket bags to be used as bird deterrents.

- Save seeds from plants in your own garden. Store them in cool dry conditions in brown paper envelopes. Remember to label them, even if you think that you will know what they all are. You don't want wallflowers growing where you expected spinach.

- Use plastic netting as a support for rapid climbers such as honeysuckle or Russian vine. Such netting is often used in the vegetable patch as a support for peas and beans but there is no real reason why it cannot be used to support purely ornamental climbers. Draped over and along fencing and properly secured so that it does not sag under the weight it provides a much cheaper form of support than wooden trellising.

- Deter snails, not with shop-bought concoctions, but with organically sound fire ash. The idea is to surround the plants you hope to protect with a generous layer of fire ash, aiming to deter the snail from crossing the barrier as it is reluctant to drag its soft body over the rough surface. Broken shells are also advocated as a free snail deterrent and both have the additional advantage of being harmless to pets.

- Another snail deterrent is liquid traps in the form of yoghurt pots filled with beer, which are then sunk to the level of the soil. The unworldly snail, attracted by the beer, comes along and falls in. These traps do of course have to be baited and emptied regularly.

- Take cuttings of softwood stems whenever you remember and for very little effort you will be repaid with new plants. This can be as simple as picking some ivy for greenery in a vase of flowers: by the time you come to change the flowers you will often find the beginning of roots showing on the ivy and the chance of another plant, if you grow it on and plant it up.

- Don't let your garden wellies rot away out of neglect; instead, make a welly rack by simply hammering long nails at suitable distances into a piece of wood attached to the garage wall. You can then suspend the boots between the nails, ensuring you always know where to find them and increasing their longevity.

- Instead of buying plant labels, make your own from strips of plastic taken from washing-up liquid bottles.

- Washing-up liquid bottles can also be used to provide collars to protect young trees.

Simply slice off top and bottom of the bottle and slit down the entire length of one side. Placed round the bottom of a tree and held in place with relatively loosely tied twine it will provide you with a cheap device for warding off the advances of rabbits.

- A rustic pole, which is often cheaper to buy than a specially planed tree stake, can make just as efficient a support and to my mind looks more attractive. Don't choose one which is too hefty or it will spoil the proportions of a young tree and remember to treat the base with a non-toxic wood preserver to increase its life.

- Use pea sticks, which can be gathered for free, instead of canes or complicated support systems to hold up your plants.

- Prevent winter losses by protecting any particularly exposed plants or those you know to be not completely hardy by draping with sacking or packing with straw or bracken. Similarly, protect plants in containers which are particularly susceptible to damage from frost. It is also worthwhile protecting the containers themselves if you believe they might crack in a severe winter. If you cannot bring them inside wrap the pot in a sacking overcoat. It may not look terrific but a few weeks protection might mean all the difference between having to fork out for a new pot in the summer and investing in new geraniums to put in the old one.

- Use old or laddered tights and stockings as tree ties. They will not chafe the bark of a tree and can be tied and retied as the tree grows.

- Buy a Christmas tree with roots. If you protect it while inside the house from the worst effects of the central heating, by keeping it in a bucket of damp peat in as cool a position as possible, you should be able to harden it off and plant it outside to increase your tree stock.

- Don't waste money on unknown quantities. Check before you buy that the plant is suitable for your garden and the location within it. At best a sun-loving plant planted in a cool damp spot is only going to grimly survive without showing the beauty of a flourishing plant and at worst it will promptly curl up its roots and die.

- Plant out tired houseplants such as polyanthus which may take on a new lease of life in the garden as they don't enjoy the warmth of the house. Similarly azaleas will do much better if after flowering in the house during winter and spring, they are allowed to enjoy the comparative coolness and freshness of the garden by having their pots sunk into a cool patch of garden soil. Pots of bulbs such as daffodils, snowdrops and hyacinth should also be planted out into the garden so they can build up their strength for next year's show. Simply dig a hole, tip the bulbs out of their container, and cover with soil to a depth of about one and a half times the length of the bulb.

- Plants can be brought in from the garden to enhance the house. A bowl of pansies still with their roots on and potted up in a clay pot can look very attractive on a cool windowsill.

- Save the heads of sunflowers to feed to the birds in winter. They love them.

- To prevent digging up plants which disappear in winter like hosta or bulbs which lie hidden under the soil, make a garden plan showing the position of all your plants and attach it to the garage wall. If it is in a readily accessible place it will act as a constant reminder which is always useful, especially if plants ever lose their labels.

- Clean pots and trays before putting them away. It pays to stack them carefully too, to avoid breakages when you try to prise clay pots apart.

- To save heating costs while still preserving plants, insulate your greenhouse with bubble film which can be attached by means of suckers and a smear of glycerine.

- Make plant protectors out of transparent plastic water bottles. Remove the base and place over your plant to deter snails and birds from feasting on the young shoots.

- Economise on Christmas decorations by making your own version of the holly wreath for the front door. Gather together evergreens from your garden such as laurel leaves, sprigs of rosemary and ivy and perhaps some small branches from a conifer. Tie them together with some stout fuse wire and festoon with a tartan ribbon. It's a lot cheaper, less funeral and more personal.

- Don't buy pot plants or shop flowers as gifts. Make your own summer posies. They will be more appreciated.

- Pot up small clumps of herbs, such as chives, marjoram and thyme in the autumn to give at Christmas when fresh herbs are at a premium. Tend the herbs inside or they will die back in the cold.

- Plan ahead for the spring by planting up bowls of bulbs for the house in the autumn. Add a little moss to the top of the pot for a finishing touch.

- Make a plant mister out of an empty plastic bottle with spray nozzle. Be sure to wash it out thoroughly first in case any chemical lingers on, which could harm your house plants.

- If your hanging baskets are at a difficult height for watering pop in a couple of ice cubes to keep the moisture up. Be sure to do it frequently though, as these baskets soon dry up on hot summer days.

- Instead of buying bags of shelled peanuts for the birds in winter ask the children to string peanuts still in their shells. Use a thimble and strong blunt needle to thread the nuts, then suspend from a tree branch. It's more fun and less expensive than buying them loose.

- Try planting seeds from the fruit bowl to make new houseplants. Try orange, lemon and even peanuts.

- Make an indoor terrarium or bottle garden out of an unwanted goldfish bowl or aquarium. Clean the glass thoroughly and use a well draining mix of peat, vermiculite and sand as compost. Choose naturally small compact plants for the best results.

- If you plan to lease an allotment try to choose one surrounded by other allotments rather than on the edge of the site. You are less likely to suffer losses from rabbits.

- Keep a special bucket in the kitchen for scraps intended for the compost heap. You are more likely to add things to your heap in this way, as you do not have to make a special trip out with every single piece of vegetable waste.

- Ask your local market traders or greengrocer for unwanted scraps of vegetable matter for the compost heap. If you wait until they are almost closing for the weekend they are usually happy to give you the waste.

- Deter aphids by spraying them with soapy water. Keep up a strict regime against them. You will have to spray repeatedly.

- Remove moss from paving by pouring on a solution of bleach. Repeat when necessary.

- Keep seed packets as a useful reminder of sowing times, spacing and height. If you are really organised you could even paste the packets onto card and keep them in a shoe box as a sort of primitive filing system.

- If you want to naturalise daffodils, buy a mixed bag of differing varieties. It will give the best effect for least cost.

- Make your own liquid fertiliser. Fill and suspend a hessian sack of manure from a wooden plank, over an old oil drum filled with water. You need to securely tie the sack and then tie the rope around the plank. Leave it to stand to allow the goodness from the manure to leak into the water. Not one recommend for the faint-hearted but I'm sure it would give you excellent fertiliser to give your crops a boost at the start of the growing season.

- Use whatever you have to make unusual plant containers; chimney pots and sinks are popular. I have even seen the cistern of a toilet being used to house fuchsia and trailing geranium. See what your local tip has to offer!

- Make friends with the local builders, who may sometimes have top soil to get rid of. Because the quantity may be fairly small they will not advertise it, but will be happy enough to give it to you if you can collect.

- Make your own pot pourris by drying petals from roses, sweet peas, pinks and tobacco plants, added to the leaves of some herbs like mint and rosemary. Dry them gently on newspaper and preserve in glass jars.

- Grow flowers with the intention of drying them for the house. Apart from the traditional favourites like statice, helichrysum and honesty, try letting onions flower and set seed as the heads look marvellous. Alternatively you could use teasels, which can look very dramatic in long vases.

- For a cheap and bold table decoration dry the head of a globe artichoke, let it open and paint it with gold or silver paint.

- If you can remove the top of an old oil drum and make puncture holes in the base, you have the start of a grand plant container. Clean out the insides, paint the exterior, and fill with a good mix of garden soil and compost. I have even seen fairly large trees being grown in such containers.

- Make a garden table out of the legs of an old sewing machine topped with a piece of hardwood.

- Make sure the handles on all your tools are smooth or you risk blistering your hands. If any handles feel rough, sand them over with abrasive paper.

- Try using oasis, beloved of floral arrangers, to take cuttings of plants like fuchsia and geranium.

- Get your children to collect caterpillars to be disposed of in hedges outside your vegetable patch.

- Save money on weedkiller by ensuring the ground is as clean as possible when initially prepared, and thereafter keep the hoe going to remove weeds as they appear.

- Instead of reaching for a spray gun just because it might be mentioned during a round-up of gardening tasks for the month, keep a watchful eye on your garden all the time. If you are really familiar with it, you will probably spot any problems in the early stages and you may be able to deal with them simply by removing a few leaves with the offending aphids or eggs on them. Chemicals should really only be the very last resort for the amateur gardener.

- Look into the possibility of using companion plants both to spur growth and deter insect attack. Well known combinations include garlic with roses and tomatoes with asparagus.

- Don't be tempted to cut costs by helping yourself to a plant or bit of a plant either from someone else's garden or in the wild. It is not good practice and could well be illegal.

- Make sure you don't kill all the insects in your garden: not all are enemies and of course some do positive good. Bees pollinate, ladybirds eat green and black fly and hoverflies eat aphids.

- Remove one side from an ordinary cardboard box and line the base and insides with tinfoil. Place your seedlings inside this lined box on a bright windowsill. The foil helps reflect as much light as possible onto the young plants.

- Don't be afraid to change things if you make a mistake. The great thing about a garden is that it is always changing and almost all-forgiving. Changing things around need not cost anything. You might simply find exchanging a few plants between sun and shade does the trick.

- Give someone a tree to mark an anniversary. It's a constant and living reminder. Do choose the tree carefully, though, to suit their needs, and help them plant it if they are unsure about going about it.

- When planting bare-root trees pop in a few bulbs at the same time. It adds interest and is very easy as you have excavated the soil anyway.

- Keep a diary to note down your successes and failures. If you write down things as you notice them it will act not only as a pleasing reminder of the changes in the garden but it will help you decide where you need to supplement planting.

- Keep planning ahead, order seeds in good time and have plants coming on for the next season.

- Be aware of which plants and seeds are poisonous and take great care especially if you have young or curious children around.

- If you keep seed from previous years sow a test batch to see if it is still potent. If more than half of your test seeds germinate they are worth sowing, if more than half fail throw them out. This saves wasting time and compost on seeds which will fail.

- Try phoning a wholesale nursery. You might find they are willing to sell young trees and shrubs much more cheaply than a garden centre.

- Use wires and eyes screwed into a wall or fence to support climbers. They are less obtrusive and cheaper than wooden trellising. A house can begin to look like a gingerbread cottage if you become over-enamoured of trellis.

- Eat what you grow. Don't, after all the effort involved, let it go to seed neglected. If you are away when a crop matures let your neighbours enjoy it – they may return the favour.

- Dead-head your flowers regularly. You may be rewarded with a second flush of flowers later in the year, or you will prolong their flowering period.

- Be patient if a hard frost strikes your plants and they look dead. It is worth waiting until mid-summer before giving up all hope of life. You don't want to discard a plant which will recover if given enough time.

- If you plan on having a gravel path or one topped with forest bark, save time on weeding by first putting down a layer of black plastic. Put your chosen topping of gravel or bark on top of the plastic, which inhibits weed growth.

- Drape old net curtains over your runner bean canes to deter birds.

- Take advantage of freebies. Visit your library to read the gardening magazines and borrow their books, listen to the radio gardeners and watch television programmes, which are often very useful in telling you what you should be doing at particular times of the year.

- Watch out for and visit local gardens on 'open' days. Sometimes a whole village will be opened up for an afternoon, allowing you to look, admire and ask questions.

- Take cuttings whenever you can. Even if you don't need them, friends will be grateful and you will always have something to offer for bring and buy sales.

- Be generous with your plants: it will pay dividends.

- Don't turn down gifts of other peoples' plants even if you already own the plant on offer – other peoples' are always so much nicer.

- Keep up to date with your tetanus injections if you do a lot of work in the garden. It is better than risking infection.

- Try coating plastic containers with a mix of paint and sand to make them look less synthetic.

- Try growing dwarf varieties of plants so that you won't have to bother with staking at all.

- Don't take into account the hours you spend in the garden or it will never be cost effective. Do it because you enjoy it.

7   CHECKLIST OF FLOWERS AND PLANTS

The following pages give a guide to the plants mentioned in this book. They are not intended as guides to cultivation but simply an indicator of plant needs. If you are attracted by any of the plants you will be quickly able to check if the position and use you have in mind will be suitable.

The plants are arranged alphabetically according to their common names.

NAME	DESCRIPTION	NEEDS

BULBS AND CORMS

NAME	DESCRIPTION	NEEDS
Autumn crocus (*Colchicum autumnale*)	Various colours, about 3–5 in (7–12 cm) high.	Plant in late summer.
Iris (*Iris* spp.)	Blue, yellow, white and orange flowers. Forms clumps with strong leaves and stems.	Plant in autumn.
Lily (*Lilium* spp.)	Various colours, flowering from summer to autumn.	Plant in autumn or winter in sun or part shade.
Grape hyacinth (*Muscari* spp.)	Spring flowering, purple-blue colour, about 10 in (25 cm) high.	Plant in groups in autumn.
Daffodil (*Narcissus* spp.)	Spring flowering from white through yellows to orange.	Plant in clumps in autumn. Achieve a natural effect by gently rolling bulbs from hand and planting where they lie.
Snowdrops (*Galanthus nivalis*)	Delicate white-green flowers from late winter to early spring. Up to about 8 in (20 cm) high.	Plant 'in the green' if possible after flowering and before tops have all died back.
Tulip (*Tulipa* spp.)	Various colours, forms and heights, flowering in late spring.	Plant in late autumn. Avoid dot planting; use in groups. Prefers sun.

FLOWERS

NAME	DESCRIPTION	NEEDS
African marigold (*Tagetes erecta*)	18–36 in (50 cm–1 m) tall. Yellows and oranges.	Flourishes easily in sun.
Aubrieta (*Aubrieta deltoidea*)	Lilac, purple, red and pink spring flowers. Grows in mats 4–6 in (10–15 cm) high.	Does best in sun. Grow from seed or cuttings.

NAME	DESCRIPTION	NEEDS
Scottish bluebell (*Campanula rotundifolia*)	About 12 in (30 cm) tall. Slender stem blooms in late summer.	Light well drained soil.
Busy Lizzie (*Impatiens*)	Long flowering, large range of colours, bright reds and oranges through to white.	Grows almost anywhere. Good for shady borders and containers. Protect from frost.
Butterfly plant (*Sedum spectabile*)	Wide flat-headed flowers, pinks and reds, about 2 ft (60 cm) high.	Sun or shade.
Candytuft (*Iberis umbellata*)	Grows to about 6 in (15 cm). Pink, lilac, purple, rose and white colours.	Sow *in situ*. Likes sun. Very easy.
Canterbury bells (*Campanula medium*)	30 in (75 cm) high. Handsome plants, pink, purple, blue and white.	Sun, rich moist soil.
Columbine (*Aquilegia* spp.)	Good range of colours, intricate flowers growing up to 3 ft (90 cm) high.	Not fussy, will grow in shade.
Cornflower (*Centaurea cyanus*)	Pretty blues and other colours from white, pink and lavender. Usually about 18 in (45 cm) high though can be taller.	Sun and well drained soil, easy.
Corn marigold (*Chrysanthemum segetum*)	Bright yellow. Grows about 9–15 in (22–40 cm). Attracts butterflies.	Attractive wildflower.
Cosmos (*Cosmos bipinnatus*)	Quick growing up to about 4 ft (1.2 m). Feathery foliage, daisy-like flowers.	Sun, part shade. Stake if exposed to the wind.
Cowslip (*Primula veris*)	Yellow, scented, traditional flower. About 9 in (23 cm) high.	Likes damp to wet soils. Easiest to start with young plants.
Cranesbill (*Geranium* spp.)	Not to be mistaken with the *Pelargonium* commonly used as a pot plant. Varied perennials, lovely blues, pink and white.	Sun or shade. Easy.
Cushion saxifrage (*Saxifraga* spp.)	Spring flowers in yellow, white, pink or red. Between 2–12 in (4–30 cm) high.	Sun or part shade. Best in gritty soil.
Delphinium spp.	Tall flowering border plant, from blue through white to purple. Up to 3 ft (90 cm) high.	Sun and a rich soil. Staking.
Forget-me-not (*Myosotis* spp.)	Usually about 7 in (18 cm) tall. Traditional blue flowers. Free seeding, can be invasive.	Sun or shade.

NAME	DESCRIPTION	NEEDS
Foxglove (*Digitalis purpurea*)	Tall growing (about 4 ft (1.2 m)) in pinks, purples and white. Poisonous. Self-seeding. Traditional plant.	Sun or part shade. Easy.
Fuchsia spp.	Various sizes, colours and forms of this tender shrub.	Sun or shade. Plenty of moisture. Frost protection.
Geranium (*Pelargonium* spp.)	Various forms and colours. Often a house plant. Can be grown from seed or cutting.	Sun, must be over wintered inside.
Greater periwinkle (*Vinca major*)	Spreading evergreen	Unfussy and can stand shade.
Lesser periwinkle (*Vinca minor*)	Blue or white flowers. Spreading.	Unfussy and easy in sun or shade.
Lobelia (*Lobelia erinus*)	Trailing and edging varieties. White, blue and pink colours. A favourite for hanging baskets.	Sun and moist rich soil.
Love-in-a-mist (*Nigella damascena*)	Similar to cornflowers in fine foliage. Can be dried.	Sun, sow outdoors.
Lupin (*Lupinus* spp.)	Traditional border plant. Good range of colours. Height varies.	Sun or shade, well drained soil.
Monkey musk (*Mimulus guttatus*)	Yellow flowers, spreading habit.	Moist soil.
Nasturtium (*Tropaeolum* spp.)	Dwarfs 10–12 in (25–30 cm). Climbers 6–10 ft (1.8–3 m). Yellows and red.	Sow outdoors in sun, poor light soil. Watch out for pests.
Pansy (*Viola* spp.)	Rich range of colours, flowers well over long period. Usually about 8–10 in (20–25 cm) tall.	Good in shade. Seed themselves around.
Pink (*Dianthus* spp.)	Blue-grey leaves, scented carnation-like flowers in white, pink and crimson.	Sun and limey soil. Needs to be replaced when middle of plant becomes bare.
Polyanthus (*Primula* spp.)	Spring flowering, huge choice of colours. Often used as pot plant.	Likes shade and moisture.
Poppy, field (*Papaver rhoeas*)	Red poppy. About 18–24 in (45–60 cm) tall. Poisonous.	Easy, attracts bees.
Poppy, oriental (*Papaver oriental*)	Large flowered, bold leaved plants. Up to about 40 in (1 m). Brilliant red, pink and white.	Sun and well drained soil. May need staking.
Poppy (Shirley hybrid)	Attractive annual poppy, mixed colours, about 2 ft (60 cm).	Best in poor sandy soil. Seed themselves.

NAME	DESCRIPTION	NEEDS
Poppy, Welsh (*Meconopsis cambrica*)	Yellow, orange flowers. About 18 in (45 cm) high.	Best in well drained soil.
Primrose (*Primula vulgaris*)	Old fashioned yellow spring flowers. Attractive on banks.	Part shade; don't let them dry out.
Rose (*Rosa* spp.)	Huge selection, varied forms for every need.	Loves the sun and well fed soil. Prune in the spring.
Scarlet sage (*Salvia splendens*)	Various strains up to about 3 ft (90 cm) high. Intense red.	Fertile, well drained soil. Sun or very light shade.
Sunflower (*Helianthus annuus*)	Yellow/orange heads. Up to 7 ft (2 m) or more. Makes good temporary hedge or screen.	Sun or light shade.
Sweet pea (*Lathyrus odoratus*)	Favourite cut flower. Delicate colours, dwarf to tall growing varieties.	Sun, fertile deeply dug ground. Dead head past flowers. Needs support.
Sweet william (*Dianthus barbatus*)	About 18 in (45 cm) tall. Flattish flowering heads. Great range of colours.	Sun or part shade.
Teasel (*Dipsacus fullonum*)	Spikey stems and heads. Up to about 6 ft (1.8 m) tall. Can be dried for the house.	Easy and unfussy.
Tobacco plant (*Nicotiana* spp.)	Pleasantly scented. White and coloured. 12–18 in (30–45 cm) high.	Sun or light shade.
Violet (*Viola odorata*)	Spring flowering, about 6 in (15 cm) high. Scented.	Part shade, fertile soil.
Virginian stock (*Malcolmia maritima*)	Quick flowering. Pinks and whites, 6–9 in (15–23 cm) high.	Very easy. Sun or light shade.
Wallflower (*Cheiranthus* spp.)	Scented, range of colours and heights, including dwarf variety.	Sun or shade. Transplants easily.
Yarrow (*Achillea* spp.)	Large family. Flat plate headed, grows between 2–5 ft (0.6–1.5 m). Mainly yellows.	Sun, can tolerate some shade.

SHRUBS AND TREES

NAME	DESCRIPTION	NEEDS
False castor oil (*Fatsia japonica*)	Broad, deeply fingered leathery leaves. Height up to 13 ft or more with a spread of 15 ft (4.5 m).	Part or full shade. Protect from frost
Cinquefoil (*Potentilla* spp.)	Dwarf and taller growing varieties. Flowers early summer to late autumn.	Sun, part shade.

NAME	DESCRIPTION	NEEDS
Canary date palm (*Phoenix canariensis*)	Large spiky leaves. Bold plant. Water frequently in summer, sparingly in winter.	House plant suitable for sheltered outdoor spot in summer.
Dogwood (*Cornus alba*)	Red stem, white variegated leaves.	Easy. Cut back in March for best stem colours.
(*Cornus stolonifera*)	Yellow stemmed. Bushy shrubs, excellent year round.	
Elder (*Sambucus nigra*)	Quick growing. Purple/black berries attract birds.	Very vigorous in fertile soil.
Forsythia spp.	Its various forms welcome spring with golden flowers. 10–15 ft (3–4.5 m) tall. Flowers on previous season's growth.	Easy, sun or light shade.
Holly (*Ilex aquifolium*)	Only female plants produce berries. Evergreen, spiky leaves. Slow growing.	Will appreciate annual manure mulch. Grows more quickly in heavy clay.
June berry (*Amelanchier* spp.)	Up to about 10 ft (3 m) high with a spread of about 5 ft (1.5 m). Offers flowers, berries and colour.	Tolerates light shade.
Mountain ash (*Sorbus* 'Joseph Rock')	Good autumn colour and yellow berries. Attractive to birds.	Easy and unfussy. Will grow in shallow soil.
Rhododendron spp.	Vast range. Most at home in light woodland.	Moist, acid soil. Feed with peat or leaf mould. Light shade.
Viburnum (*Viburnum bodnantense*)	9–12 ft (2.75–3.6 m) high. Upright stems, white pink scented flowers on bare branches during winter.	Easy and unfussy.
(*Viburnum burkwoodii*)	Evergreen, scented white flowers in winter.	Grows almost anywhere.
(*Viburnum tinus*)	Evergreen up to 10 ft (3 m) high. Dark green leaves, winter flowering.	Easy and unfussy.
Witch hazel (*Hamamelis* spp.)	Sweet smelling twisted yellow flowers on bare branches in winter. Slow growing.	Best near house to enjoy scent. Unfussy, light shade.
Yucca spp.	Large sword-like leaves growing from a trunk. Water frequently in summer, sparingly in winter.	Like most house plants, benefits from a summer airing.

NAME	DESCRIPTION	NEEDS

CLIMBERS

NAME	DESCRIPTION	NEEDS
Chinese wisteria (*Wisteria sinensis*)	Usually blue flowers, delicate leaves. Can grow very tall.	Sun, wind protection. Well fed soil. Best to buy containered.
Clematis spp.	Wide choice of colour and form. Good for climbing up and through roses or trees.	Keep roots in shade and head in sun.
Honeysuckle (*Lonicera* spp.)	Sweet smelling climber, can be very vigorous. Deciduous and evergreen forms, flowering from spring to autumn.	Unfussy sun or part shade. Propagate from cuttings from late summer to autumn.
Ivy (*Hedera* spp.)	Self clinging climber, many varieties, colours and forms.	Unfussy, fast growing when established.

HERBS

NAME	DESCRIPTION	NEEDS
Borage (*Borago officinalis*)	Star shaped blue flowers, bristly leaves. Up to 3 ft (90 cm) high. Flowers can be used for food decoration.	Unfussy, might need staking. Seeds freely.
Catmint (*Nepeta* spp.)	Grey, green scented leaves, delicate lavender flowers.	Sun and well drained soil.
Chervil (*Anthriscus cerefolium*)	Feathery leaves about 10 in (25 cm) tall. Aniseed flavour, self-seeding.	Light shade.
Chives (*Allium schoenoprasum*)	Clumps of purple headed onion type leaves. About 12 in (30 cm) high. Perennial/purple-pink flowers, useful for salads.	Sun or tolerates light shade. Likes moist soil.
Florence fennel	Crisp 'bite', aniseed flavour.	Light rich soil, water if dry.
Garlic (*Allium sativum*)	White and pink forms. Useful in cooking.	Plant cloves in autumn in sun, in light well drained soil.
Hyssop (*Hyssopus officinalis*)	Perennial small shrub with attractive purple blue flowers. Attracts bees and butterflies.	Best in well drained soil. Replace after about 4 years.
Lavender (*Lavandula* spp.)	Blue, grey scented foliage. From about 2 ft (60 cm) to over 3 ft (90 cm) tall.	Favours well drained sunny position.
Marjoram (*Origanum vulgare*)	Perennial neat attractive white-pinkish flowers. Useful for meat and salads. Can be potted up for use indoors in winter.	Good in sun and well drained soil.

NAME	DESCRIPTION	NEEDS
Mint (*Mentha* spp.)	Large family, can be invasive.	Loves moisture. May do well to plant in a bottomless bucket, sunk in soil to contain roots.
Parsley (*Petroselinum crispum*)	Green leaves used as decoration and in sauces.	Start from seed. Sun or part shade.
Rosemary (*Rosmarinus officinalis*)	About 4 ft (1.3 m) high. Shrub with scented needle-like leaves and pale lilac/blue flowers. Useful with lamb, chicken and stews.	Can tolerate some shade. Roots easily from cuttings.
Rue (*Ruta graveolens*)	Attractive, evergreen, yellow flowers in summer. Seeds itself.	Sun but not fussy. Can be invasive.
Sage (*Salvia officinalis*)	Perennial, various colours. Can be chopped in salads.	Best in well drained light soil and sun. Replace after about 4 years.
Thyme (*Thymus* spp.)	Various forms and colours. Can be potted for inside use in winter.	Sun and well drained soil.

VEGETABLES

Asparagus	Perennial. Must wait for third season before cutting.	Deeply dug and well fed soil.
Cabbage	Possible to get year round supply from wealth of different varieties.	Well drained fertile soil.
Carrot	Early and main crops. Short, stumpy and long finger varieties.	Best on light soil.
Cauliflower	Many types maturing at different times.	Moisture retentive fertile soil.
Courgette	Large golden flowers, sprawling leaves.	Needs well fed soil, may have to pollinate flowers by hand.
Globe artichoke	Grows up to about 5 ft (1.5 m).	Well dug and fed soil. Protect from frost.
Lettuce	Hearting and non-hearting varieties. Sow in succession.	Can stand light shade. Appreciates well dug and fed soil.
Mange-tout, Sugar Snap peas	Edible pods, different varieties.	Best in deep rich soil. Water when dry.
Potato	Very early, early and maincrop varieties. Maturing from 80–100 days, maincrop four weeks later.	Free draining soil. Water when necessary. Don't let potatoes dry out.

NAME	DESCRIPTION	NEEDS
Radish	Sow continuously from spring to autumn.	Sandy soil is ideal. Keep well watered.
Runner bean	Decorative red or white flowers. Grows up to about 6 ft (1.8 m).	Good soil. Start inside in late spring or outdoors in summer. Tie onto canes to encourage growth.
Spinach	Edible leaves, quick growing, sow in succession.	Rich soil able to retain moisture. Can grow in light shade.
Tomato	Both greenhouse and outdoor varieties. Start seed in warmth.	Fertile, well drained soil. Feeding.

FRUIT

Blackcurrant	Fruiting bushes placed about 5 ft (1.5 m) apart.	Clean soil, lots of compost and shelter from wind.
Redcurrant	Can be grown as bush, cordon or espalier.	Sun or part shade. Dislikes water logging.
Rhubarb	Coloured edible stalks, large crinkly leaves. Can be handsome garden decoration.	Sun and well fed soil. Can be forced for early picking by covering the plants in December with bucketful of straw.
Strawberry	Vast number of varieties, different fruiting times, size and flavour.	Protection from birds.

8 SEASONAL DIARY

Rather than create a calendar of gardening tasks month by month, in the following diary I try to indicate seasonal needs as regional variations and the vagaries of the weather can make a strict timetable difficult to adhere to.

As you get to know your garden these tasks will become automatic and natural but until you are confident be guided by those around you with more experience. Rather than rush ahead, be patient as you cannot easily compress the natural growth cycle. If you plant seeds in open ground a month before every-one else you are unlikely to have stolen a march on them at harvest time. It is more probable that your seeds will have rotted in the ground because of the cold and wet.

Look to see what others are doing, and consider the weather. Don't, just because an article recommends sowing seed in April, feel obliged to do so. If your ground is wet and soggy, wait a few weeks for it to dry out and warm up. It may mean planting in May but this won't matter if the growing conditions are better.

SPRING

Check for winter damage in the garden. Remove broken branches and those damaged by wind and snow.
Check that tree ties have not worn and broken and that the roots of roses and newly planted specimens have not been slackened by the frost.
After the frosts are past, carry out any necessary construction work.
Make sure the mower is working for the first cut of the year. Set the blades at their highest level for a long cut.
Clean the greenhouse and cold frame, ready to accommodate this year's plants.
Check cloches and put them in position. Make your first open ground sowing offering cloche protection if needed.
Buy more seed trays if you need them and check your stocks of bamboo canes for the summer.

Plan your vegetable patch.

Finish planting bare-root plants if you have not already done so.
Take a few softwood cuttings.

Sow or turf areas of grass. Start first sowings of seed indoors.

Prune roses where necessary.

Cultivate by spreading manure or other soil enricher if you failed to do this in the autumn. Dig over and prepare new border areas and prepare all ground to be planted. Mulch established plants.

Harden off bedding plants.

Consider successful groupings of bulbs which might be replicated elsewhere in the garden and also note gaps in the border which could be brightened by bulbs next year. Buy new pots or hanging baskets if you need them for a summer display.

SUMMER

Ensure you do not let hanging baskets and containers dry out, by watering daily.
To avoid disappointment, check the children's paddling pool for leaks before getting it out for them for the first time.

Plant out hardened off bedding plants, and tired houseplants such as polyanthus. Give other houseplants a breath of fresh air during the day and a refreshing shower in summer rain.
Take cuttings of plants whenever you can.

Continue sowing seeds indoors and out.

Weed paved areas.
Keep weeds at bay in the borders by regular hoeing and close work with a hand fork.

Cut grass regularly. Edge the lawn for extra neatness.

Water plants as necessary.

Stake tall plants before they need it.

Pick and enjoy summer vegetables and fruit daily.
Cut posies for friends without gardens.

Tie in climbing plants and dead head flowers regularly to encourage a long display.

Consider visiting open gardens so that you can take note of good ideas and particulary stunning plants and arrangements.
Invite friends round for leisurely lunches to enjoy your garden.
Hold impromptu barbeques whenever the weather merits – summer seems too short always to plan get-togethers.

AUTUMN

Check that you don't encourage pests and disease by leaving rotting vegetable debris lying around, if it will break down, put it into the compost – if not bag it up and take it to the refuse tip.

Remove tired bedding plants and think about plants for the spring.

Plant first bulbs for the spring.
Divide and multiply herbaceous plants.

Sow or turf lawns.
Allow plants to seed around; you might be surprised and delighted by the result.

Cut the grass as long as it is growing.

Bring in non-hardy plants.

Rake and aereate the grass.

Pick green tomatoes if in danger of being frosted, and ripen indoors in a dark drawer. Alternatively roll up your sleeves and make a few jars of green tomato chutney for the coming Harvest Festival.
Harvest herbs for drying. Try to do this on a dry morning before the sun is up in the sky and not when the plants are wet after heavy rain.
Freeze any glut crops if you can.
Pick suitable seedheads and flowers for winter arrangements.

Gather fallen leaves to make leaf mould and put bruised windfall fruit which are too damaged to eat in the compost. Tidy away any canes no longer needed and begin digging over the vegetable patch.
Order manure and set aside a weekend for digging and mulching.

Consider the successes and failures of the past season. Look for improvement and treat yourself to a new plant. A container-grown shrub would be ideal.

WINTER

Check the mower and give it a service; store the wheelbarrow upended if it is not housed in a shed or garage. Run an oiled rag over the face of other tools.

Check fencing is proof against winter gales.

Clean pots and trays and put away. Similarly, check over bamboo canes and store for the winter.

Clean out and check over the greenhouse and cold frame.

Make sure compost heaps are secure and covered to keep the heat in.

Remove heavy snowfalls from plants to stop the weight causing damage.

Plan for the next year. Study catalogues to see what is on offer. Look at the bones of your garden. Could you use more winter colour, more climbers, more evergreens? Aim to have year-round interest.

Pay attention to indoor plants: try something you have not attempted to grow before.

Plant bare root plants when the weather and ground will allow.

Take hard wood cuttings.

Finish off bulb planting, remembering some for the house.

Tidy up tools and hang up those you will not need for a season.

Protect or bring indoors any containers you think might suffer frost damage. Make sure any slightly tender plants still outside are offered as much protection as possible with straw or sacking.

Try covering up unused patches of ground with sheets of polythene weighted by stones to keep the worst of the weather out. You can remove such sheeting to expose the ground to the positive effects of the frosts as they help break up roughly dug ground. When the weather becomes wet again simply put the sheets back in place.

Don't damage your lawn unnecessarily by walking on it when it is waterlogged or frozen.

Pick greenery for the house: foliage can be as effective as flowers.

Don't be too impatient to start work again in the garden. Enjoy life indoors while you can, as there is nothing to be gained from starting too soon.

GLOSSARY

acid – describes peaty soil which suits plants like heathers and rhododendrons.

aerate – to pierce the lawn with the tines of a fork to allow air in; helps drainage.

annual – a plant which grows, matures and dies within a growing season.

bare-root – describes a plant lifted from the ground, not one grown in a container.

bed – area designated for plants.

bedding plant – plants put in for a temporary display.

biennial – plant which is started from seed in one year for flowering the next. Takes two growing seasons from start to finish.

bog plant – plant particularly suited to very moist conditions.

broadcast – method of sowing seed, scattering rather than sowing in rows.

bonemeal – fertiliser made from powdered bones.

climber – plant which grows upwardly. Some are self clinging like ivy others need support and tying up.

cloche – various kinds. Used to keep soil dry and to bring on your plants, protected from the worst of the weather.

cold frame – sort of mini greenhouse, to protect and bring on plants.

compost, garden – the result of well decayed garden matter. Should be dark brown and crumbly.

compost – growing medium for seeds, cuttings and plants.

cordon – single stemmed tree trained to shape.

cutting – means of propagating a plant by taking a piece from the mother plant.

dead head – removal of past flowers.

dibber – a tool to make small planting holes.

dot plant – plant used singly, usually in a formal planting scheme.

drill – furrow in which to sow seed.

espalier – tree trained and pruned to have branches coming out at right angles from the stem.

F1 hybrid – exceptional plant or seed bred for its best features. Does not breed true.

fertiliser – plant or soil enricher.

forcing – encouraging early growth by protection and/or heat. Commonly used with reference to rhubarb.

friable – what good soil should be: brown and crumbly.

germination – when seed bursts into life.

grow-bag – bag of compost in which plants can be grown. Often used for tomatoes.

half hardy – seed which is best begun in warmth, will die in frost and needs winter protection.

hardy – cold resistant.

herbaceous perennial – a plant which dies back in winter but grows again next year, hopefully increasing in size.

insecticide – chemical used to kill insects.

leaf mould – rotted leaves, useful as a mulch or improving soil generally.

loam – ideal soil.

manure – cow, horse or pig; well rotted, it is a great soil improver.

mole – tool for making holes suitable for posts.

mulch – weed suppressant layer of matter on top of soil.

naturalise – often refers to bulbs in long grass. Informal planting in harmonious surroundings.

organic matter – not chemical or man made, but derived from living organisms, for example manure, compost and leaf mould.

pesticide – chemical used to kill pests.

pollination – transfer of pollen from male to female parts of flower.

potash – essential for plant growth, present in fertiliser.

pricking out – sorting and spacing out of seedlings.

propagation – increase of plants, for example by root division, cuttings or seed.

riddle – a large sieve-like object for sifting soil.

rootball – earth and roots of a plant.

root division – means of increasing plants by splitting up roots.

scarify – a serious rake over to remove moss and thatch from grass.

secateurs – useful hand tool to snip and cut stems and branches.

softwood cutting – sappy top-most part of shoot taken for rooting.

sprinkler – spray attachment for garden hose.

spring rake – fine tined springy rake for scarifying grass.

standard – usually refers to a rose, but anything grown on a bare stem of upwards of about four feet.

tap root – long strong growing root.

tender – describes non-hardy plant which needs protection.

terrarium – indoor bottle garden.

thatch – matted growth in a lawn.

tilth – fine top layer of soil.

variegated – two tone markings on leaves.

vermiculite – used in potting compost, sterile substance made from expanded mica.

BIBLIOGRAPHY

Evans, Hazel, *The Patio Garden*, Windward, 1985

Genders, Roy, *The Cottage Garden Year*, Croom Helm, 1986

Godfrey, Leslie, *The Reluctant Gardener*, Windward, 1983

Hunt, Peter, FLS, *100 Best Herbaceous Plants*, The Garden Book Club, 1963

Hunt, Peter, Ed. *Gardening for All*, Octopus, 1978

Kiaer, Eigil, *Garden Planning and Planting*, Blandford Press Ltd., English Edition, 1976

Rose, Graham, *The Low Maintenance Garden*, Windward, 1983

Sawyer, Allan, *The Plant Buyer's Directory*, Ebury Press, 1986

Stevenson, Violet, *The Wild Garden*, Windward, 1985

Evergreen Trees and Shrubs/The Time-Life Encyclopedia of Gardening, Series Editor Robert M Jones, Time-Life Books Inc., 1978

The Gardening Encyclopedia, Windward, 1982

Lawns and Ground Covers/The Time-Life Encyclopedia of Gardening, Series Editor Robert M Jones, Time-Life Books Inc., 1978

The Royal Horticultural Society's Concise Encyclopedia of Gardening Techniques, Editor in Chief Christopher Brickell, Mitchell Beazley, 1983

INDEX

Figures in **bold** refer to page numbers of illustrations